**PROFESSIONAL
RESOURCES**

D0814898

The Four-Blocks™
Literacy Model

Systematic Sequential Phonics They Use:

For Beginning Readers of Any Age

by

Patricia Cunningham

Editors
Joey Bland
Tracy Soles

Cover
Jeff Thrower

Systematic Sequential Phonics They Use
Table of Contents

Systematic Sequential Phonics They Use
Introduction

I began my teaching career in 1965 in a first grade classroom in Key West, Florida. In later years, I taught fourth grade and worked as a special reading teacher, a curriculum coordinator, and a district director of reading. In recent years, I have taught undergraduate elementary education classes at Wake Forest University in Winston-Salem, North Carolina. Throughout those years, I have been concerned (my closest friends would say "obsessed") with two issues. "How do we find alternative ways of teaching reading to those students for whom learning to read is a daily struggle?" and "How do we teach phonics so that students not only learn the sounds for the letters, but actually use what they know when they need to use it—as they are reading and writing?"

Most of my ideas for alternative teaching strategies were born out of necessity. Take for example the ideas of displaying high-frequency words on the classroom wall, providing daily practice with them, and requiring these words to be spelled correctly in all writing. I came up with those ideas after watching countless children with years of "regular instruction" experience who could not tell **went** from **want**, and who spelled **they—t-h-a-y** and **said—s-e-d**. I came up with Making Words out of my frustration with children who could tell you that the "**e** on the end made the vowel long," but couldn't figure out new words with long vowel sounds and **e**'s on the end, and children who spelled **same—s-a-m** and **bite—b-i-t**. So I got little letter cards and we made words, and once the children had made **Sam** or **bit**, I asked them to add a letter to change it to **same** or **bite**. Lo and behold, struggling children who practiced the Word Wall words daily and were required to spell them correctly could learn to read and spell the high-frequency words, including words like **they** and **said** which are not spelled logically. And they could learn to use their phonics knowledge when they needed it to manipulate letters to spell words,

figure out the secret word, and read and spell the transfer words that are a critical part of every Making Words lesson.

By the summer of 1989, I knew that activities such as Word Wall and Making Words could indeed help struggling students learn to decode and spell words and use that knowledge as they were reading and writing. But I didn't have a clear sense of why these activities worked, nor was there a research base to support them. That summer, I read Marilyn Adam's *Beginning to Read* (1990). As I read, I realized why these activities worked and that there was indeed a research base about how students learned words that supported these activities. By the time I finished reading *Beginning to Read*, I had decided to write a book for teachers. That book became *Phonics They Use*, and if you are intrigued by the research base I mentioned, you will find a summary of this research in the last chapter of *Phonics They Use, 3rd ed.* (2000).

Spurred by *Phonics They Use*, the *Making Words* series Dottie Hall and I published in 1994 and 1997, and the recent *Month-by-Month Phonics* series (1997-1998), teachers around the country began using Word Walls and Making Words as part of their phonics and spelling instruction. Their response was enthusiastic, and I thought I was done trying to figure out how to teach phonics that students, especially struggling readers, would actually use.

In the summer of 2000, however, teachers began to express concern about having to give up their Word Walls, Making Words, and other multilevel phonics activities because they were being mandated to use "systematic" phonics that followed a "scope and sequence." I argued, "Phonics instruction that includes Word Walls and Making Words *is* systematic. And you can plug the lessons in so that they do follow a scope and sequence, if necessary." In spite of my protests, I knew that many teachers were going to have to give up these phonics activities that were working for them and move to programs that were clearly systematic and sequential.

In mid-June, as I was packing to go on the dream-of-a-lifetime Alaskan cruise, I suddenly began to wonder if teachers could "have their cake and eat it, too." In other words, would it be possible to structure Making Words lessons so that they followed a typical phonics scope and sequence? Could you get the Word Wall words out of the Making Words lessons? Could you cover all the skills necessary in the right order and still have secret words and sort out rhymes for transfer words? I got my trusty Franklin Spelling Ace®, which when you enter a word will list all the other words that can be made from the letters in the word you entered. Then, I began to play around. By the time my husband and I left for the cruise, I was hooked. I stuffed my Franklin Spelling Ace® and my laptop computer into my large purse. As I winged my way across the country, I made up lessons. We boarded the cruise ship and I set up my computer. Each morning my husband would get up around 5:00 to find me working away with my Franklin Spelling Ace® and my computer. (It was daylight in Alaska, and it was 9:00 AM Eastern time!) He would shake his head, pick up the phone and order room service coffee. I had a great time on the cruise, and I didn't work all the time, but early in the morning, or when things were boring, I made up lessons for what has become this book.

The Lessons

This book contains 140 lessons that teach all the common phonics patterns in the most commonly accepted sequence. The lessons are arranged in five-lesson cycles. The first four lessons in each cycle are Making Words lessons. Children are given 5-10 letters with which to make 10-12 words, as well as a "secret word," which can be made using all the letters. If no one gets the secret word in one minute, the teacher gives them clues to help them figure it out. Once the words are made, students sort the cards on which the words are written for certain patterns. These sorted patterns are then used in the Transfer step of the lesson. In the first 30 lessons, the Sort step is for beginning sounds and the Transfer step has students deciding which of the words they made begin like a new word. In the remainder of the lessons, the students sort for rhyming words and they transfer by using the rhyming words they made to read two new rhyming words. Some lessons also have students sorting for blends (**bl**, **br**, **st**, etc.) and related words (**small/smaller**; **skin/skinny**).

The fifth lesson in each cycle reviews some of the words made in the first four lessons and calls for adding five of the words made to the Word Wall. Starting with lesson six, each daily lesson ends with the teacher calling out five of the Word Wall words for the students to chant, write, and check, thus providing a daily review of these critical words.

Following the 140 lessons are some review activities. These can be used after the 140 lessons are completed or at any point when you feel the students need some review. (If you do some of these before all words are added to the wall, you will need to adjust the suggested activity for the words you currently have on the wall.) The review activities include both the Word Wall words and all the phonics/spelling strategies taught.

The Scope and Sequence

There is no research to support any particular order of teaching phonics elements. There is, however, a tradition of teaching certain elements in a certain order, and that traditional sequence was used to structure these lessons. All phonics elements with enough regularity to be useful are included in the lessons. The phonics elements are taught in a Making Words lesson and a word representing that element is added to the Word Wall as a key word reminder. When teaching the letter sounds to students, it is important to avoid using jargon as much as possible. Children get very confused by terms such as blend, digraph, short vowels, long vowels, r-controlled vowels. (One first grader explained to me that it was easy to tell the short vowels from the long vowels—the short vowels were the lowercase ones and the long vowels were the capitals!) As teachers, we do use the words vowels and consonants. Rather than referring to digraphs and blends, we talk about beginning letters and teach students that beginning letters include all the letters up to the vowel. We teach the sounds by using the keyword example—**a** as in **at**, **a** as in **make**, **ar** as in **car**. Children, particularly struggling readers, respond better when we tell them that the vowel in a word they are trying to decode has the "**a** sound in the word **at**" than when we tell them to use the "short sound of **a**." The traditional terminology is used here to make sure the connection is made to traditional phonics, but we do not use this terminology with the students.

Here are the phonics elements and the general order in which they are taught.

Most Useful Consonants:

b c d f g h j k l m n p r s t w

Short Vowel Patterns:

a (as in at); e (as in end); i (as in it); o (as in on); u (as in up)

Digraphs:

ch sh th ck

Long Vowel Patterns:

o (as in no); e (as in he); i-e (as in ride); igh (as in night); o-e (as in those); u-e (as in use); ay (as in day); ai (as in rain); ee (as in see); ea (as in eat); oa (as in float)

R-controlled vowels:

ar (as in car); or (as in for); er (as in her); ir (as in girl); ur (as in hurt)

Other Common Vowel Patterns:

oi (as in oil); oy (as in boy); aw (as in saw); au (as in because); al (as in walk); ou (as in cloud); ow (as in now and slow); oo (as in zoo and look); ew (as in new); y (as in my and very)

Less Useful Consonants/Digraphs:

v; x; y; z; wh; qu; c (as in centers); g (as in gym)

Blends:

bl br cl cr dr fl fr gl gr pl pr sc sk sl sm sn st sw tr

Endings:

s; ed; ing; er (person); er (more); est (most); ly

The Word Wall

The Word Wall is a critical component of *Systematic Sequential Phonics They Use.* Five words, made by the students during the previous four lessons, are added as part of every fifth lesson. These words include high-frequency words and an example for each phonics element taught. Words are displayed on the wall under the letter of the alphabet with which they begin and in the order introduced in the lessons. (They are not alphabetized by the second letter, but are simply placed under the letter with which they begin.) Because it is so easy to become confused, different colors of paper are used for words beginning with the same letters or each word is outlined in a different color. A star or sticker is placed on words with the same rhyming patterns. This will help students spell at least five other rhyming words and teach them how to use these starred words to spell other words. In addition to the classroom Word Wall, the students are given a take-home Word Wall each week which contains all the words on their classroom wall. (Reproducible, Take-Home Word Walls are on pages 158-185.) On the next page is a list of the 140 words. If the word is a key word for a particular element, that element is indicated in parentheses. Starred words have useful rhyming patterns. We put a clue next to **too (too big)** and **two (2)** to distinguish them from **to,** as well as next to **their (their car)** to distinguish it from **there**.

after
all*
am*
an*
and*
are
as
at* (a)
be
because (au)
before
big* (b)
biggest (est most)
black* (bl ck)
boy* (oy)
brother (br)
but*
can*
car* (c ar)
centers (c/s sound)
children (ch)
cloud (cl ou)
come
could
creatures (cr)
day* (d ay)
do
dry* (dr)
eat* (ea)
end* (e)
float* (fl oa)
for (f or)
friend (fr)
from
get*
girl (ir)
glad* (gl)
go (g)
good
green (gr)
gym (g/j sound)
had* (h)
has
have
he (e)
her (er)
here
him*
how*
hurt (ur)
I
if
in*
is
it* (i)
jump* (j)
jumping (ing)
kittens (k)
like*
little
look* (l oo)
make* (a-e)
me (m)
more*
my* (y)
new* (ew)
nice*
night* (igh)
not* (n)

now* (ow)
of
oil (oi)
old*
on (o)
or
our
over
pet* (p)
player (pl er person)
probably (pr ly)
question (qu)
rain* (ai)
red* (r)
ride* (i-e)
run*
said
same* (s)
saw* (aw)
scare (sc)
see* (ee)
she (sh)
six (x)
skate* (sk)
slow* (sl ow)
smart* (sm)
smaller (er more)
snake* (sn)
so
some
sport* (sp)
stop* (st)
stopped (ed)
sweater (sw)
tell*
that*
the
their (car)
them
then*
there
they
things* (s)
this (th)
those* (o-e)
to
too (big)
train* (tr)
two (2)
under
up (u)
us
use (u-e)
very (v y)
walk (al)
want (w)
was
we
went*
were
what
when* (wh)
where
who
why*
will*
with
you (y)
your
zoo (z oo)

Making Words Lessons

Making Words lessons are hands-on, minds-on manipulative activities in which students discover how our English spelling system works. They are given a limited number of letters (5-10 for the lessons in this book) and then guided to make words in a sequence that helps them discover patterns. The order in which they make words is very important and should not be random. Children need to learn that predictable things happen to a word when you change the first letter, the last letter, or the vowel. They need to realize that the order of letters is crucial, and that when they "move the letters around" **rat** becomes **tar** and then **art**. They need to learn that you change **bit** to **bite** and **not** to **note** by adding that very important **e**. Likewise, **ran** becomes **rain** and **cot** becomes **coat** when vowels you don't hear are added.

Unlike other Making Words lessons, these lessons are tied to a phonics scope and sequence. The first lessons help students learn the sounds for the most common consonants and for the short vowels. Only words that follow those patterns are included and students get lots of practice "stretching out words" and listening for the sounds they hear and the order of those sounds. Later lessons introduce the more complex consonant and vowel patterns.

Every Making Words lesson has three steps. In the Making step, students manipulate letters to make words as directed by the teacher. They make the words using little letter cards with lowercase letters on one side and uppercase on the other side. (Reproducible letter cards can be found on pages 191-192.) Vowels are distinguished from the consonants in some way—either by putting them on a different colored card or drawing a distinctive shape, such as a circle, around the vowels. The letter **y** is a different color or enclosed in a different shape since it can be both a vowel and a consonant. In addition to the little letter cards the students manipulate, the teacher has a larger set of letters which fit in a pocket chart and can be seen by all the students.

Pacing is very important to the engagement of students during a Making Words lesson. We tell them what word to make, and put the word in a sentence unless it is such a well-known word that no sentence is needed. We quickly find someone who has made it correctly, and send that student to make it with the pocket chart letters. We **do not wait** for everyone to get the word made. Most students are still making the word as the student is going to make it with the big letters. Once the word is made with the big letters, we ask everyone to fix their own version if it needs fixing, then move quickly to the next word. Because most words are made by making small changes to the previous word, students quickly learn to fix an incorrect word so that they can make the next word. The last word in every Making Words lesson is the secret word, a word that can be made using all the letters. After just a few lessons, students start anticipating the teacher's question, "Does anyone have the secret word? I am coming to see if anyone has it, and if not, I will give you some clues." From the moment the students get their little letters, they are trying to figure out the secret word. Trying to figure out how **all** the letters could spell a word engages their minds in some wonderful thinking about how letters, sounds, and words work.

Once the secret word is made using the big letters, we begin the second step of a Making Words lesson, Sorting the words according to patterns. To do this we make word cards, one card for each of the 10-12 lesson words. These cards are placed in the pocket chart and the teacher guides the students to sort words with the same beginning letters, rhyming words, and related words. I have tried to recycle words, using them in more than one lesson. There are 112 Making Words lessons, each with 10-12 words for the students to make. However, there are only 815 word card words, including transfer words because words are used more than once. You can make your word cards on index cards, file them alphabetically, and save them for future lessons. They are also reused in many of the review activities.

Once the words are sorted, we do the third (and probably most important) step. We help the students use the words they have made and the patterns they have sorted to read two new words. "Pretend you are reading and you come to this word. Don't say it. Who can go and put it with the rhyming words that will help you figure it out?" Once the two transfer words are lined up under the rhyming words the class made, we pronounce all the words. Children learn how the letter patterns will help them when they come to an unknown word. It is much easier to teach students phonics than it is to teach them to use the phonics they know as they read. The transfer step is critical and makes all the rest of our efforts worthwhile.

After a Making Words lesson is done, many teachers give students a take-home sheet with the letters from the lesson across the top and blocks for writing words. The students write capital letters on the back and then cut the letters apart. They manipulate the letters to make words and then write them in the blocks. They can make the same words made in class or come up with new ones. When we write the letters on the top, we write them in alphabetical order, vowels first followed by the consonants, so as not to give away the secret word. The student, of course knows the secret word but people at home (parents, grandparents, big brothers) don't, and students love seeing how long it takes their families to figure out the secret word. Most students report that if their families can't get the secret word, they give them some clues just like the teacher does at school. (A reproducible Making Words Take-Home sheet on which you can write letters is found on page 186.)

Making Words Take Home Sheet									
a	e	e	c	h	r	t			

My Hopes and Fears for This Book

In publishing this book, I feel a little as if I am sending my precious child off to school and he is going to be taught by one of the teachers I trained. I am equally afraid that she will not do anything I taught her or that she will try to do everything I taught her without monitoring how well it is working for my child and the rest of his classmates. This book does contain explicit instructions for each lesson because systematic instruction requires that. There is an example sentence for each word (except for words used many times previously) because it is hard to make up good sentences on the spot. (I thought this was true before I started making up sentences and am totally convinced after making up approximately 1200 sentences!) My hope is that you will be guided by the spirit of the lessons and not the exact words. I tried to include words I thought most students would have heard before, but have included a few lesser-known words in order to get two sets of rhymes or a particular beginning sound. If I have included a word none of your students will have heard before, leave that word out. I avoided "bad" or "violent" words, but if you find a word offensive or think your students will "titter" about it, leave it out. Use your children's names in the sentences and make the sentences fit your neighborhood. (If the example sentence says, "I saw (NAME) at the grocery store." and all your students shop at Piggly Wiggly®, substitute Piggly Wiggly® for grocery store.) Children will be more engaged and pay better attention if the sentences are about them and their world.

My greatest fear for this book is that someone will pick it up and think they have a "total" reading program. Phonics is an important part of any balanced reading program, but it is only one part. Children need to be guided in the comprehension of what they read. They need to read for sustained periods of time, using materials they choose. They also need to use what they are learning about letters and sounds as they write things they want to tell. There are a number of ways to provide students with a balanced literacy program. The one I have worked on most is called The Four-Blocks™. [For more about The Four-Blocks™, see *The Teacher's Guide to the Four-Blocks™*, by Cunningham, Hall, and Sigmon (1999) and *Classrooms that Work* by Cunningham and Allington (1999).] In the Four-Blocks™ framework, students spend 30-40 minutes each day in Guided Reading in which they learn how to comprehend all kinds of text. Four-Blocks students also spend 30-40 minutes in Self Selected Reading in which they participate in a teacher-read-aloud and then read books they have chosen. The Four-Blocks™ framework also calls for 30-40 minutes of Writing and 30-40 minutes of Working With Words. *Systematic Sequential Phonics They Use* is one way of providing the instruction in the quarter of the literacy instructional time we give to Working with Words.

My greatest hope for this book is that it will allow teachers to provide active hands-on, minds-on phonics instruction that will stimulate children's minds, while still meeting the requirements of systematic and sequential phonics instruction. I also hope that teachers and students will view phonics not as something to be dreaded and endured, but as a wonderful exploration into how words work. Enjoy!

Lessons 1-5
Letters and Sounds: a (as in at); b d h l m n p s t

Lesson 1

Letters: a d n s t
Words: at an and Dan tan ant sat sad sand stand

Name letters and their common sounds: Before beginning to make words, have the students hold up each letter, name it, and say its common sound. Have the students show both the lowercase and capital letters.

Make words: Have the students make these words, then send one student to make each word using the big letters. DO NOT wait for everyone to make the word before sending someone up. Keep the lesson fast-paced and the students will pay better attention. When the word is made with the big letters, ask everyone to check their words and fix them if necessary.

1. Take 2 letters and make **at**. <u>We are **at** school.</u>
2. Take the **t** away and add a different letter to make **an**. <u>I ate **an** apple.</u>
3. Add a letter to **an** and you can spell **and**. <u>I like apples **and** bananas.</u>
4. Now we are going to do a trick with **and**. Move the letters in **and** around so that they spell **Dan**. Stretch out **Dan** and listen for where you hear the **D** and the **a** and the **n**. (Look for a student who has **Dan** spelled with a capital letter **D**, and send that student to make **Dan** with the big letters.) <u>My cousin's name is **Dan**.</u>
5. Take the **D** away and add a letter to spell **tan**. <u>I got a **tan** at the beach.</u>
6. Now let's do the "move the letters around" trick with **tan** to spell **ant**. Stretch out **ant** with me and listen for where you hear the sounds. <u>The **ant** is tiny.</u>
7. Let's start over and make another 3-letter word, **sat**. <u>The boy **sat** down.</u>
8. Take the **t** away, add another letter, and you can spell **sad**. <u>He was very **sad**.</u>
9. Now we are going to spell a 4-letter word. Add 1 letter to **sad** and you can spell **sand**. Let's all say **sand** and listen for the letter we need to add. <u>She digs in the **sand**.</u>
10. The last word in every lesson is the secret word. Add 1 letter to **sand** and you can spell another word. I am going to look and see if anyone has figured out the secret word. (Give them no more than a minute to try to figure it out and then say a sentence with the secret word. <u>Everyone **stand** up.</u>) Have someone make **stand** with the big letters.

Sort: Collect the letters, then read with the students all the words in the pocket chart. Next, have them sort the words into columns according to their first letter.

at	sat	Dan	tan
an	sad		
and	sand		
ant	stand		

Transfer: Say some words in sentences and have the students repeat the words and decide what letter they begin with.

dog top sun add apple teacher doctor sister

Lesson 2

Letters: a m p s t
Words: am at mat sat Sam Pam map Pat past stamp

Name letters and their common sounds: Before beginning to make words, have the students hold up each letter, name it, and say its common sound. Have the students show both the lowercase and capital letters.

Make words: Have the students make these words, then send one student to make each word using the big letters. DO NOT wait for everyone to make the word before sending someone up. Keep the lesson fast-paced and the students will pay better attention. When the word is made with the big letters, ask everyone to check their words and fix them if necessary.

1. Take 2 letters and make **am**. I **am** your teacher.
2. Take the **m** away and add a different letter to make **at**. We are **at** school.
3. Add a letter to **at** and you can spell **mat**. Wipe your feet on the **mat**.
4. Take the **m** away and add a letter to spell **sat**. I **sat** on the couch.
5. Take the **t** away and add a letter to spell **Sam**. I have a friend named **Sam**. I am looking for someone who has **Sam** spelled with a capital letter to make **Sam** with the big letters.
6. Take the **S** away and add a letter to spell another name, **Pam**. **Pam** is Sam's twin sister.
7. Now let's do the "move the letters around" trick with **Pam** to spell **map**. I need a **map** to help me find places.
8. Take 3 letters and spell one more name, **Pat**. **Pat** is Sam's and Pam's little sister.
9. Now we are going to spell a 4-letter word. Turn the **P** over to its lowercase side and add 1 letter to **pat** and you can spell **past**. She walked **past** the library. Let's all say **past** and listen for the letter we need to add.
10. The last word in every lesson is the secret word. You have one minute to try to arrange all your letters to spell the secret word. (Give them no more than a minute to try to figure it out, then give them a clue. You use this to mail a letter.) I need a **stamp** to mail this letter. Have someone make **stamp** with the big letters.)

Sort: Collect the letters, then read with the students all the words in the pocket chart. Next, have them sort the words into columns according to their first letter.

at	sat	mat	past
am	Sam	map	Pam
	stamp		Pat

Transfer: Say some words in sentences, and have the students repeat the words and decide what letter they begin with.

pet mop see Al after mother pencil supper

Lesson 3

Letters: a b l s t
Words: Al as at sat bat tab stab bats last blast

Name letters and their common sounds: Before beginning to make words, have the students hold up each letter, name it, and say its common sound. Have the students show both the lowercase and capital letters.

Make words: Have the students make these words, then send one student to make each word using the big letters. DO NOT wait for everyone to make the word before sending someone up. Keep the lesson fast-paced and the students will pay better attention. When the word is made with the big letters, ask everyone to check their words and fix them if necessary.

1. Take 2 letters and make **Al**. My brother's name is **Al**. What kind of letter will the name **Al** begin with?
2. Turn the A to the lowercase side and take the **l** away and add a different letter to make **as**. I am **as** tall **as** my sister.
3. Take the **s** away and add another letter to spell **at**. We start school **at** 8:30.
4. Add a letter to **at** and you can spell **sat**. We **sat** together on the bus.
5. Take the **s** away and add a letter to spell **bat**. We need a **bat** to play baseball.
6. Now let's do the "move the letters around" trick with **bat** to spell **tab**. Pull the **tab** to open the can.
7. Add a letter to **tab** to spell **stab**. Be careful you don't **stab** yourself with those scissors.
8. Move the letters in **stab** around and you will have **bats**. Let's all say **bats** and listen for where we hear the letters. We saw **bats** in the cave.
9. Now we are going to spell one more 4-letter word, **last**. I don't like to be **last** in line. Let's all stretch out **last** and listen for the letters we need.
10. Now it's time for the secret word. Figure out where to add the **b** to **last** and you can spell the secret word. Did you hear that loud **blast**? Have someone make **blast** with the big letters.

Sort: Collect the letters, then read with the students all the words in the pocket chart. Next, have them sort the words into columns according to their first letter.

at	sat	last	bat	tab
as	stab		bats	
Al			blast	

Transfer: Say some words in sentences and have the students repeat the words and decide what letter they begin with.

tip bus light add soap lady baby table

Lesson 4

Letters: a d h n s
Words: an as sad had has Dan and sand hand hands

Name letters and their common sounds: Before beginning to make words, have the students hold up each letter, name it, and say its common sound. Have the students show both the lowercase and capital letters.

Make words: Have the students make these words, then send one student to make each word using the big letters. DO NOT wait for everyone to make the word before sending someone up. Keep the lesson fast-paced and the students will pay better attention. When the word is made with the big letters, ask everyone to check their words and fix them if necessary.

1. Take 2 letters and make **an**. I need **an** umbrella.
2. Take the **n** away and add a different letter to make **as**. That huge dog was **as** big **as** a horse.
3. Now take 3 letters and spell **sad**. I was **sad** when my old dog died.
4. Take the **s** away and add a letter to spell **had**. We **had** pizza for lunch.
5. Take the **d** away and add a letter to spell **has**. (NAME) **has** brown hair.
6. Now let's spell the name, **Dan**. **Dan** drives the school bus. Who remembers what kind of letter we need for a name?
7. Move the letters in **Dan** around and turn the **D** over to spell **and**. (NAME) **and** (NAME) are friends.
8. Add a letter at the beginning of **and** you will have **sand**. We love to dig in the **sand**.
9. Take the **s** away and add a different first letter to spell **hand**. Raise your **hand** to answer the question.
10. Now it's time for the secret word. Figure out where to add the **s** to **hand** and you can spell the secret word. Wash your **hands** before lunch. Have someone make **hands** with the big letters.

Sort: Collect the letters, then read with the students all the words in the pocket chart. Next, have them sort the words into columns according to their first letter.

an	sad	Dan	had
as	sand		has
and			hand
			hands

Transfer: Say some words in sentences and have the students repeat the words and decide what letter they begin with.

hot dig soup ax summer dinosaur happy animal

Lesson 5

Word Wall Words: am and at had has
Secret Words: stand stamp blast hands
Letters and Sounds for Review: a (as in at); b d h l m n p s t

To review the letters and sounds, the big letters for each secret word are put in the pocket chart and students are invited to come and make words they remember from each lesson. (Students do not have their little individual letters.) Students should not try to make all the words from each lesson, but do have them make each secret word. Be sure they make the five words that will be added to the Word Wall.

Review

1. Put the big letters **a, d, n, s,** and **t** in the pocket chart. Let students come and make any words they can. If no one makes **and**, ask someone to come and make it. Show them the Word Wall card for **and**. Tell them that **and** is a word we use a lot and will be one of the first words added to the Word Wall.
2. Remove the **d** and **n** and add **m** and **p**. Again, let students come and make some words. Be sure they make **am** and show them the Word Wall card for **am**.
3. Remove the **m** and **p** and add **b** and **l**. Again, let students come and make some words. Be sure they make **at** and show them the Word Wall card for **at**.
4. Remove the **b, l,** and **t** and add **n, h,** and **d**. Again, let students come and make some words. Be sure they make **had** and **has** and show them the Word Wall cards for **had** and **has**.

Word Wall

1. Place the words on the wall, having the students say each word and use each word in a sentence.
2. Point to each word and have the students chant its spelling three times in a rhythmic manner ("**h-a-d, had; h-a-d, had; h-a-d, had**").
3. Have the students write each word as you model good writing on the board or overhead projector. Model and talk about correct letter formation as you write each word.
4. Have the students check their words by pointing to each letter and saying it aloud. Have them fix any words that need fixing.
5. If possible, give everyone a copy of the Take-Home Word Wall (page 158).

Lessons 6-10
Letters and Sounds: i (as in it); c f g r w

Lesson 6

Letters: i g n s w
Words: is in win wig wigs wins sing wing wings swing

Name letters and their common sounds: Before beginning to make words, have the students hold up each letter, name it, and say its common sound. Have the students show both the lowercase and capital letters.

Make words: Have the students make these words, then send one student to make each word using the big letters. DO NOT wait for everyone to make the word before sending someone up. Keep the lesson fast-paced and the students will pay better attention. When the word is made with the big letters, ask everyone to check their words and fix them if necessary.

1. Take 2 letters and make **is**. (NAME) **is** a fast runner.
2. Take the **s** away and add a different letter to make **in**. We are **in** school.
3. Add a letter to spell **win**. We want our team to **win**.
4. Take the **n** away, add a letter, and you can spell **wig**. Do you wear a **wig**?
5. Add a letter to spell **wigs**. I know a lady who has ten **wigs**.
6. Change just 1 letter and spell **wins**. Our team **wins** almost every week.
7. Start over with your letters and spell another 4-letter word, **sing**. We **sing** every morning.
8. Change 1 letter and you can spell **wing**. The bird broke its **wing**.
9. Today there are 2 secret words. Add the **s** to **wing** in 2 different places and see what words you can make. (Give them a minute to try to figure them out and then say sentences with the secret words.) I like to **swing**. A bird has **wings**. Have two students make **swing** and **wings** with the big letters.

Sort: Collect the letters, then read with the students all the words in the pocket chart. Next, have them sort the words into columns according to their first letter.

is	sing	win
in	swing	wins
		wig
		wigs
		wing
		wings

Transfer: Say some words in sentences and have the students repeat the words and decide what letter they begin with.

if wet sort will wagon iguana water soda

Word Wall: Call out the five words from the Word Wall. Have the students chant them, write them, and check them. Emphasize letter names, sounds, and word formation as you do this each day. Remind them that the starred words will help them spell lots of rhyming words. Say the words **bad, land, ham,** and **cat**. Then, have the students tell you the words they rhyme with.

Lesson 7

Letters: i f g s t
Words: is if it sit fit fits fist sift gift gifts

Name letters and their common sounds: Before beginning to make words, have the students hold up each letter, name it, and say its common sound. Have the students show both the lowercase and capital letters.

Make words: Have the students make these words, then send one student to make each word using the big letters. DO NOT wait for everyone to make the word before sending someone up. Keep the lesson fast-paced and the students will pay better attention. When the word is made with the big letters, ask everyone to check their words and fix them if necessary.

1. Take 2 letters and make **is**. Fruit **is** good for you.
2. Take the **s** away and add a different letter to make **if**. I will come **if** I can.
3. Take the **f** away and add a different letter to make **it**. **It** is my birthday.
4. Add a letter to spell **sit**. **Sit** on the couch.
5. Take the **s** away and add a letter to spell **fit**. Try on the shoes to see if they **fit**.
6. Add a letter to spell **fits**. This shoe **fits** fine.
7. Now let's do the "move the letters around" trick with **fits** to spell **fist**. I can make a **fist** with my hand.
8. Do the "move the letters around" trick again and change **fist** to **sift**. You **sift** flour to make cookies.
9. Take the **s** away and add 1 letter to spell **gift**. I need to buy a **gift** for the birthday party.
10. I bet you can get the secret word. (Give them a minute to try to figure it out and then say a sentence with the secret word.) I got a lot of **gifts** for my birthday. Have someone make **gifts** using the big letters.

Sort: Collect the letters, then read with the students all the words in the pocket chart. Next, have them sort the words into columns according to their first letter.

is	sit	fit	gift
if	sift	fits	gifts
it		fist	

Transfer: Say some words in sentences and have the students repeat the words and decide what letter they begin with.

go food in song Indian garbage forest super

Word Wall: Call out the five words from the Word Wall. Have the students chant them, write them, and check them. Emphasize letter names, sounds, and word formation as you do this each day. Remind them that the starred words will help them spell lots of rhyming words. Say the words **band, sad, bat,** and **jam.** Then, have the students tell you the words they rhyme with.

Lesson 8

Letters: i g n r s t
Words: is in it sit rig ring grin sing sting string

Name letters and their common sounds: Before beginning to make words, have the students hold up each letter, name it, and say its common sound. Have the students show both the lowercase and capital letters.

Make words: Have the students make these words, then send one student to make each word using the big letters. DO NOT wait for everyone to make the word before sending someone up. Keep the lesson fast-paced and the students will pay better attention. When the word is made with the big letters, ask everyone to check their words and fix them if necessary.

1. Take 2 letters and make **is**. (NAME) **is** happy.
2. Take the **s** away and add a different letter to make **in**. We were **in** the library.
3. Take the **n** away and add another letter to spell **it**. **It** will be a great day.
4. Add a letter to **it** and you can spell **sit**. Let's **sit** on the rug.
5. We're going to spell one more 3-letter word, **rig**. A big truck is called a **rig**.
6. Add a letter to **rig** to spell **ring**. The bell will **ring** soon. Let's stretch out **ring** and listen for what letter to add and where to add it.
7. Move the letters in **ring** around and you can spell **grin**. The boy had a big **grin** on his face.
8. Let's spell one more 4-letter word, **sing**. We all love to **sing**.
9. Now we are going to add 1 letter to **sing** to spell **sting**. Bees will **sting** you. Let's all stretch out **sting** and listen for the letter we need.
10. I bet you can get the secret word. (Give them a minute to try to figure it out and then say a sentence with the secret word.) I tied the bundle of sticks with **string**. Have someone make **string** with the big letters.

Sort: Collect the letters, then read with the students all the words in the pocket chart. Next, have them sort the words into columns according to their first letter.

is	sit	ring	grin
in	string	rig	
it	sing		
	sting		

Transfer: Say some words in sentences and have the students repeat the words and decide what letter they begin with.

sip	ran	if	goat	saddle	itchy	garden	rabbit

Word Wall: Call out the five words from the Word Wall. Have the students chant them, write them, and check them. Emphasize letter names, sounds, and formation as you do this each day. Remind them that the starred words will help them spell lots of rhyming words. Say the words **sat, ram, sand,** and **mad**. Then, have the students tell you the words they rhyme with.

Lesson 9

Letters: a i c g m n p
Words: in pin nip nap map man can cap camp camping

Name letters and their common sounds: Before beginning to make words, have the students hold up each letter, name it, and say its common sound. Have the students show both the lowercase and capital letters. Make sure the students notice they have two vowels, and review these vowel sounds.

Make words: Try to keep the lesson fast-paced. Quickly send someone to make the word with the big letters. Remind the students to check their words and fix them if necessary.

1. Take 2 letters and make **in**. I saw (NAME) **in** the grocery store.
2. Add a letter to make **pin**. **Pin** this on your shirt.
3. Move the letters in **pin** to spell **nip**. A puppy will **nip** at your feet.
4. Take the **n** away and add a letter to spell **nap**. If I'm tired, I like to take a **nap**.
5. Take the **n** away and add a letter to spell **map**. A **map** helps us find places.
6. Take the **p** away and add a letter to spell **man**. The **man** was fixing the car.
7. Take the **m** away and add a letter to spell **can**. We **can** read.
8. Take the **n** away and add a letter to spell **cap**. I am wearing my new **cap**.
9. Add 1 letter to **cap** to spell **camp**. I like to hike and **camp** in the woods. Let's stretch out **camp** and listen for what letter we need to add to **cap**.
10. Now it's time for the secret word. Add the rest of your letters to **camp** and see what you can spell. Today's secret word is a hard one because we have seven letters to use. (Give them a minute to try to figure it out and then say a sentence with the secret word.) **Camping** is lots of fun. Have someone make **camping** with the big letters.

Sort: Collect the letters, then read with the students all the words in the pocket chart. Next, have them sort the words into columns according to their first letter.

in	can	man	pin	nap
	camp	map		nip
	camping			
	cap			

Transfer: Say some words in sentences and have the students repeat the words and decide what letter they begin with.

cat	me	no	pick	paper	music	never	cookies

Word Wall: Call out the five words from the Word Wall. Have the students chant them, write them, and check them. Emphasize letter names, sounds, and formation as you do this each day. Remind them that the starred words will help them spell lots of rhyming words. Say the words **Sam, hand, dad,** and **fat**. Then, have the students tell you the words they rhyme with.

Lesson 10

Word Wall Words: if in it is can
Secret Words: swing wings gifts string camping
Letters and Sounds for Review: i (as in it); a (as in at); c f g m n p r s t w

To review the letters and sounds, the big letters for each secret word are put in the pocket chart and students are invited to come and make words they remember from each lesson. (Students do not have their little individual letters.) Students should not try to make all the words from each lesson, but do have them make each secret word. Be sure they make the five words that will be added to the Word Wall.

Review

1. Put the letters **i, g, n, s,** and **w** in the pocket chart. Let students come and make any words they can. If no one makes **is** and **in**, ask someone to come and make them. Show them the Word Wall cards with **is** and **in**. Tell them that **is** and **in** are words we use a lot and will be added to the Word Wall.
2. Remove the **w** and **n** and add **f** and **t**. Again, let students come and make some words. Be sure they make **if** and **it** and show them the Word Wall cards for **if** and **it**.
3. Remove the **f** and add **r** and **n**. Again, let students come and make some words.
4. Remove the **s, r,** and **t** and add **a, c, m,** and **p**. Again, let students come and make some words. Be sure they make **can** and show them the Word Wall card for **can**.

Word Wall

1. Place the words on the Word Wall, having the students say each word and use each word in a sentence.
2. Help the students notice the stars on **can, in,** and **it**. Tell them that these words have stars because they will help them spell lots of rhyming words.
3. Point to each new word and have the students chant its spelling three times in a rhythmic manner (**"c-a-n, can; c-a-n, can; c-a-n, can"**).
4. Have the students write each new word as you model good writing on the board or overhead projector. Model and talk about correct letter formation as you write each word.
5. Have the students check their words by pointing to each letter and saying it aloud. Have them fix any words that need fixing.
6. If possible, give everyone a copy of the Take-Home Word Wall (page 159).

Lessons 11-15
Letters and Sounds: u (as in up); j k

Lesson 11

Letters: u k n r s t
Words: us sun run rut nut nuts stun rust trunk trunks

Name letters and their common sounds: Before beginning to make words, have the students hold up each letter, name it, and say its common sound. Have the students show both the lowercase and capital letters.

Make words: Have the students make these words and send one student to make the word with the big letters. Keep the lesson fast-paced. When the word is made with the big letters, ask everyone to check their words and fix them if necessary.

1. Take 2 letters and make **us**. Mom took **us** to the mall.
2. Take 3 letters and make **sun**. The **sun** is shining.
3. Change just the first letter and you can spell **run**. (NAME) can **run** fast.
4. Change just the last letter and you can spell **rut**. There was a huge **rut** in the road.
5. Change just the first letter and you can spell **nut**. The squirrel was eating a **nut**.
6. Add 1 letter to **nut** to spell **nuts**. Squirrels eat lots of **nuts**.
7. Move the letters in **nuts** around and you can spell **stun**. The news I am going to tell you will **stun** you.
8. We're going to spell 1 more 4-letter word, **rust**. The old car was covered with **rust**.
9. Now we are going to spell a 5-letter word, **trunk**. An elephant has a **trunk**. Let's all stretch out **trunk** and listen for the letters we need.
10. I bet you can get the secret word. (Add your last letter to **trunk**. What do you have? Yes. When you add **s** to **trunk**, you have **trunks**.) Elephants' noses are called **trunks**.

Sort: Collect the letters, then read with the students all the words in the pocket chart. Next, have them sort the words into columns according to the word's first letter.

us	sun	run	nut	trunk
	stun	rut	nuts	trunks
		rust		

Transfer: Say some words in sentences and have the students repeat the words and decide what letter they begin with.

| up | rug | seat | next | tacos | under | number | sister |

Word Wall: Call out the five words added in lesson 10—**if, in, it, is,** and **can.** Have the students chant them, write them, and check them. Emphasize letter names, sounds, and formation. Remind them why **can, in,** and **it** have stars. Say the words **man, sit, win,** and **hit.** Have the students decide the words they rhyme with.

Lesson 12

Letters: i u g j m n p

Words: up in pin pig jig jug mug gum jump jumping

Name letters and their common sounds: Before beginning to make words, have the students hold up each letter, name it, and say its common sound. Have the students show both the lowercase and capital letters.

Make words: Have the students make these words and send one student to make the word with the big letters. DO NOT wait for everyone to make the word before sending someone up. Ask everyone to check their words and fix them if necessary.

1. Take 2 letters and make **up**. I woke **up** early.
2. Now spell one of our Word Wall words, **in**. Go **in** the house.
3. Add a letter to **in** and you can spell **pin**. She wore a pretty **pin** on her sweater.
4. Change just the last letter to spell **pig**. We saw a baby **pig**.
5. Change just the first letter to spell **jig**. We danced a **jig**.
6. Now, change just the vowel and spell **jug**. Sometimes milk comes in a **jug**.
7. Change the first letter and spell **mug**. I drink coffee from a **mug**.
8. Now let's do the "move the letters around" trick with **mug** to spell **gum**. (NAME) likes to chew bubble **gum**.
9. Now we are going to spell a 4-letter word, **jump**. (NAME) likes to **jump** rope. Let's all stretch out **jump** and listen for the letters we need.
10. Keep **jump** and add your remaining 3 letters to make the secret word. You have one minute to try to arrange all your letters to spell the secret word. (NAME) was **jumping** over the rocks.

Sort: Collect the letters, then read with the students all the words in the pocket chart. Next, have them sort the words into columns according to their first letter.

up	in	pin	mug	gum	jump
		pig			jumping
					jig
					jug

Transfer: Say some words in sentences and have the students repeat the words and decide what letter they begin with.

jog   good   us   man   jogging   umbrella   goblins   paper

Word Wall: Choose five words from the Word Wall for review. Have the students chant them, write them, and check them. Emphasize letter names, sounds, and formation.

Lesson 13

Letters: e u g j l n s
Words: us Gus leg lug jug jugs lugs slug legs jungles

Name letters and their common sounds: Before beginning to make words, have the students hold up each letter, name it, and say its common sound. Have the students show both the lowercase and capital letters.

Make words: Have the students make these words and send one student to make the word using the big letters. DO NOT wait for everyone to make the word before sending someone up. Have everyone check their words and fix them if necessary.

1. Take 2 letters and make **us**. Look at **us**.
2. Add a letter to **us** to spell the name, **Gus**. Gus is not here today. Do you remember what kind of first letter we use to spell names?
3. Now spell another 3-letter word, **leg**. The girl fell and broke her **leg**.
4. Change the vowel and you can spell **lug**. It was hard to **lug** the heavy box.
5. Change just the first letter to spell **jug**. We bought a **jug** of milk.
6. Add a letter to **jug** to spell **jugs**. We bought two **jugs** of milk.
7. Change just the first letter to spell **lugs**. (NAME) **lugs** all the heavy boxes.
8. Move the letters in **lugs** around and you will have **slug**. Let's all say **slug** and listen for where we hear the letters. A **slug** is a small, slimy animal.
9. Now we are going to spell one more 4-letter word, **legs**. I have two **legs**.
10. Now it's time for the secret word. It's a hard one and if no one gets it in a minute, I will give you some clues. (It starts with a **j**. The second letter is a **u**. It is a place where tigers and monkeys live.) Monkeys and tigers live in **jungles**.

Sort: Collect the letters, then read with the students all the words in the pocket chart. Next, have them sort the words into columns according to their first letter.

us	jug	leg	Gus	slug
	jugs	lug		
	jungles	lugs		
		legs		

Transfer: Say some words in sentences and have the students repeat the words and decide what letter they begin with.

| get | lamp | juice | sip | until | jaguar | laundry | garage |

Word Wall: Choose five words from the Word Wall for review. Have the students chant them, write them, and check them. Emphasize letter names, sounds, and formation.

Lesson 14

Letters: a i b b r s t
Words: is it at sat sit bit bat rat brat rabbits

Name letters and their common sounds: Before beginning to make words, have the students hold up each letter, name it, and say its common sound. Have the students show both the lowercase and capital letters.

Make words: Have the students make these words and send one student to make the word with the big letters. DO NOT wait for everyone to make the word before sending someone up. Ask everyone to check their words and fix them if necessary.

1. Let's start by making one of our Word Wall words, **is**. <u>(NAME) **is** working hard.</u>
2. Let's make another Word Wall word, **it**. <u>**It** was raining.</u>
3. Now make another Word Wall word, **at**. <u>I saw (NAME) **at** the mall.</u>
4. Add a letter to spell **sat**. <u>We **sat** together in the cafeteria.</u>
5. Change the vowel and you can spell **sit**. <u>**Sit** down.</u>
6. Change the first letter and you can spell **bit**. <u>The dog **bit** the boy.</u>
7. Change the vowel and you can spell **bat**. <u>Can I use your **bat**?</u>
8. Change the first letter and you will have **rat**. <u>I saw a big **rat**.</u>
9. Add 1 letter to **rat** to spell **brat**. <u>Sometimes my little cousin is a **brat**.</u>
10. Now it's time for the secret word. It's a hard one, but try to use all your letters and spell 1 word. (You may want to give them some clues. It's an animal. It starts with **r**. This animal eats carrots.) <u>**Rabbits** eat carrots.</u>

Sort: Collect the letters, then read with the students all the words in the pocket chart. Next, have them sort the words into columns according to their first letter.

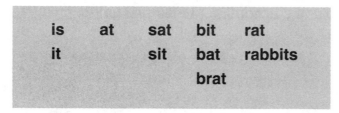

is	at	sat	bit	rat
it		sit	bat	rabbits
			brat	

Transfer: Say some words in sentences and have the students repeat the words and decide what letter they begin with.

big read six ask icky barber rescue attic

Word Wall: Choose five starred words from the Word Wall for review. Have the students chant them, write them, and check them. Say a word that rhymes with each of the starred words and have them tell you the word it rhymes with.

Lesson 15
Word Wall Words: run jump jumping up us
Secret Words: trunks jumping jungles rabbits
Letters and Sounds for Review:
a (as in at); i (as in it); u (as in up); b g j k l m n p r s t

To review the letters and sounds, the big letters for each secret word are put in the pocket chart and students are invited to come and make words they remember from each lesson. (Students do not have their little individual letters.) Students should not try to make all the words from each lesson, but do have them make each secret word. Be sure they make the five words that will be added to the Word Wall.

Review

1. Put the big letters **u, k, n, r, s,** and **t** in the pocket chart. Let students come and make any words they can. If no one makes **us** and **run,** ask someone to come and make them. Show them the Word Wall cards for **us** and **run.**
2. Remove the **k, r, s,** and **t** and add **i, g, j, m** and **p.** Again, let students come and make some words. Be sure they make **up, jump,** and **jumping** and show them the Word Wall cards for **up, jump,** and **jumping.**
3. Remove all the letters except the **u, g,** and **j;** add **e, l, n,** and **s.** Again, let students come and make some words.
4. Remove all the letters except the **s,** and add **a, i, b, b, r,** and **t.** Again, let students come and make some words.

Word Wall

1. Place the words on the Word Wall, having the students say each word and use each word in a sentence.
2. Help the students notice the stars on **run** and **jump.** Tell them that these words have stars because they will help them spell lots of rhyming words.
3. Point to each new word and have the students chant its spelling three times in a rhythmic manner (**"r-u-n, run; r-u-n, run; r-u-n, run"**).
4. Have the students write each new word as you model good writing on the board or overhead projector. Model and talk about correct letter formation as you write each word.
5. Have the students check their words by pointing to each letter and saying it aloud. Have them fix any words that need fixing.
6. If possible, give everyone a copy of the Take-Home Word Wall (page 160).

Lessons 16-20
Letters and Sounds: e (as in end)

Lesson 16

Letters: e d n p s
Words: Ed Ned den pen end ends dens pens send spend

Name letters and their common sounds: Before beginning to make words, have the students hold up each letter, name it, and say its common sound. Have the students show both the lowercase and capital letters.

Make words: Have the students make these words and quickly send one student to make the word with the big letters. When the word is made with the big letters, ask everyone to check their words and fix them if necessary.

1. Take 2 letters and make **Ed**. I have an Uncle **Ed**. (Find someone who used a capital **E** to make **Ed** with the big letters.)
2. Add 1 letter to **Ed** and you can spell another name, **Ned**. Ned is a nice name.
3. Turn the capital **N** over, move the letters around, and you can spell **den**. Lions live in a **den**.
4. Change just the first letter and you can spell **pen**. She wrote the letter with a **pen**.
5. Let's spell one more 3-letter word, **end**. I didn't like the **end** of the movie.
6. Add just 1 letter and spell **ends**. The party **ends** at 4:00.
7. Move the letters in **ends** around and you can spell **dens**. Lots of lions need lots of **dens**.
8. Change 1 letter and you can spell **pens**. Everyone likes to write with **pens**.
9. Let's spell one more 4-letter word, **send**. I am going to **send** my friend a birthday card. Let's all say **send** and stretch it out to hear all the letters.
10. Keep the letters in **send** where they are, add your other letter, and see if you can figure out the secret word. (Give them a minute to try to figure it out and then say a sentence with the secret word.) I love to **spend** money.

Sort: Collect the letters, then read with the students all the words in the pocket chart. Next, have them sort the words into columns according to their first letter.

Ed	Ned	den	pen	send
end		dens	pens	spend
ends				

Transfer: Say some words in sentences and have the students repeat the words and decide what letter they begin with.

edge   park   door   name   donut   sister   enter   nation

Word Wall: Call out the five words added in lesson 15—**up, us, run, jump,** and **jumping**. Have the students chant them, write them, and check them. Emphasize letter names, sounds, and formation. Remind them that the starred words will help them spell lots of rhyming words. Say the words **fun, bump, dump,** and **sun**. Have the students tell you the words they rhyme with.

Lesson 17

Letters: e n p s t
Words: pen ten net pet pest pets nets nest sent spent

Name letters and their common sounds: Before beginning to make words, have the students hold up each letter, name it, and say its common sound. Have the students show both the lowercase and capital letters.

Make words: Have the students make these words and quickly send one student to make each word using the big letters. When the word is made with the big letters, ask everyone to check their words and fix them if necessary.

1. Take 3 letters and make **pen**. I lost my favorite **pen**.
2. Change just the first letter to make **ten**. I have **ten** fingers.
3. Move the letters around to change **ten** into **net**. Hit the ball over the **net**.
4. Change just the first letter to spell **pet**. I wish I had a **pet** pony.
5. Add a letter to spell **pest**. Sometimes, my puppy is a **pest**. Let's stretch out **pest** to see what letter to add where.
6. Do the "move the letters around" trick to turn **pest** into **pets**. My neighbor has 5 **pets**.
7. Change the first letter to spell **nets**. People catch butterflies in **nets**.
8. Do the "move the letters around" trick again and change **nets** to **nest**. The mother bird built a **nest** for her eggs.
9. Move the letters around again and spell **sent**. I **sent** a present to my nephew.
10. Add the **p** to **sent** and you can spell the secret word. (Give them a minute to try to figure it out and then say a sentence with the secret word.) I **spent** all my money on the present.

Sort: Collect the letters, then read with the students all the words in the pocket chart. Next, have them sort the words into columns according to their first letter.

pen	ten	net	sent
pet		nets	spent
pets		nest	
pest			

Transfer: Say some words in sentences and have the students repeat the words and decide what letter they begin with.

peach	song	test	night	noodles	party	toaster	silly

Word Wall: Choose five words from the Word Wall for review. Have the students chant them, write them, and check them. Emphasize letter names, sounds, and formation as you do this each day.

Lesson 18

Letters: e i b g g s t
Words: is it sit set bet bit big beg best biggest

Name letters and their common sounds: Before beginning to make words, have the students hold up each letter, name it, and say its common sound. Have the students show both the lowercase and capital letters.

Make words: Have the students make these words and quickly send one student to make the word using the big letters. When the word is made with the big letters, ask everyone to check their words and fix them if necessary.

1. Take 2 letters and make the Word Wall word, **is**. <u>(NAME) **is** smiling.</u>
2. Let's make another Word Wall word, **it**. <u>Where did you get **it**?</u>
3. Add a letter to **it** and you can spell **sit**. <u>I want to **sit** here.</u>
4. Change the vowel and you can spell **set**. <u>We got a new **set** of dishes.</u>
5. Change the first letter and make **bet**. <u>I **bet** you can spell **bet**.</u>
6. Change the vowel and you can spell **bit**. <u>Give me just a little **bit**.</u>
7. Change the last letter and you can spell **big**. <u>I ate a **big** cookie.</u>
8. Change the vowel to spell **beg**. <u>My dog will sit up and **beg**.</u>
9. Now take 4 letters and spell **best**. <u>Saturday is the **best** day of the week.</u> Let's all stretch out **best** and listen for the letter we need.
10. The secret word is a hard one today. Try to make it, and then I will give you some clues. (Start by making **big** again. Add letters to spell a word that means really big.) <u>I got the **biggest** piece of cake.</u>

Sort: Collect the letters, then read with the students all the words in the pocket chart. Next, have them sort the words into columns according to their first letter.

is	sit	big
it	set	beg
		bit
		bet
		best
		biggest

Transfer: Say some words in sentences and have the students repeat the words and decide what letter they begin with.

sun bell if boat saddle itchy bacon surprise

Word Wall: Choose five words from the Word Wall for review. Have the students chant them, write them, and check them. Emphasize letter names, sounds, and formation as you do this each day.

Lesson 19

Name letters and their common sounds: Before beginning to make words, have the students hold up each letter, name it, and say its common sound. Have the students show both the lowercase and capital letters. Make sure the students notice they have two vowels and review those vowel sounds.

Make words: Keep the lesson fast-paced. Quickly send someone up to make each word using the big letters. Remind everyone to check their words and fix them if necessary.

1. Let's start with a 3-letter word, **ten**. I go to bed at **ten** o'clock.
2. Move the letters around to make **net**. You can catch fish in a **net**.
3. Add just 1 letter to spell **nest**. The squirrel was in the **nest**.
4. Move the letters around to spell **sent**. I got mad and **sent** him home.
5. Change the first letter to spell **tent**. You can sleep outside in a **tent**.
6. Change just 1 letter to spell **test**. I passed the driving **test**.
7. Now we are going to start again and use 4 letters to spell **skin**. Your **skin** protects your body. Let's stretch out **skin** and listen for the letters we hear.
8. Move the letters around and you can spell **sink**. Wash your hands in the **sink**.
9. Add 1 letter to **sink** to spell **stink**. Garbage that sits out in the sun will **stink**. Let's stretch out **stink** and listen for the letter we need to add to **sink**.
10. Now it's time for the secret word. It's a hard one today because we have seven letters to use. In a minute, I will give you some clues. (Start your word with the **k**. The word is what we call baby cats.) Baby **kittens** are so cute.

Sort: Collect the letters, then read with the students all the words in the pocket chart. Next, have them sort the words into columns according to their first letter.

net	sent	tent	kittens
nest	sink	test	
	stink	ten	
	skin		

Transfer: Say some words in sentences and have the students repeat the words and decide what letter they begin with.

king toes see nine needle turtle kitchen size

Word Wall: Choose five starred words from the Word Wall for review. Have the students chant them, write them, and check them. Say a word that rhymes with each of the starred words and have the students decide the word it rhymes with.

Lesson 20
Word Wall Words: big biggest end kittens pet
Secret Words: spend spent biggest kittens
Letters and Sounds for Review: e (as in end); i (as in it); b d g k n p s t

To review the letters and sounds, the big letters for each secret word are put in the pocket chart and students are invited to come and make words they remember from each lesson. (Students do not have their little individual letters.) Students should not try to make all the words from each lesson, but do have them make each secret word. Be sure they make the five words that will be added to the Word Wall.

Review

1. Put the letters **e, d, n, p,** and **s** in the pocket chart. Let students come and make any words they can. If no one makes **end,** ask someone to come and make it. Show them the Word Wall card for **end.**
2. Remove the **d** and add **t**. Again, let students come and make some words. Be sure they make **pet** and show them the Word Wall card for **pet.**
3. Remove the **n** and **p**; add **b, g, g,** and **i**. Again, let students come and make some words. Be sure they make **big** and **biggest** and show them the Word Wall cards for **big** and **biggest**.
4. Remove the **b, g,** and **g**; add **k, n,** and **t**. Again, let students come and make some words. Be sure they make **kittens** and show them the Word Wall card for **kittens**.

Word Wall

1. Place the words on the Word Wall, having the students say each word and use each word in a sentence.
2. Help the students notice the stars on **pet, big,** and **end**. Remind them that these words have stars because they will help them spell lots of rhyming words.
3. Point to each new word and have the students chant its spelling three times in a rhythmic manner ("**b-i-g**, **big**; **b-i-g**, **big**; **b-i-g**, **big**").
4. Have the students write each new word as you model good writing on the board or overhead projector. Model and talk about correct letter formation as you write each word.
5. Have the students check their words by pointing to each letter and saying it aloud. Have them fix any words that need fixing.
6. If possible, give everyone a copy of the Take-Home Word Wall (page 161).

Lessons 21-25
Letters and Sounds: o (as in on); o (as in no); -ck

Lesson 21

Letters: o d n p s
Words: so no on Don nod pod pods nods pond ponds

Teach letter sounds: Before beginning to make words, have the students hold up each letter, name it, and say its common sound. Tell the students that the vowel **o** can have the sound you hear at the beginning of **on** and at the end of **no**. Have the students practice both sounds for **o**.

Make words: Have the students make these words and send one student to make each word with the big letters. Keep the lesson fast-paced. When the word is made with the big letters, ask everyone to check their words and fix them if necessary.

1. Take 2 letters and make **so**. You all did **so** well.
2. Change the first letter and make **no**. No, I don't want to go.
3. Move the letters around and you can spell **on**. What's **on** TV?
4. Add a letter and you can spell **Don**. I went to the mall with my friend, **Don**.
5. Turn the **D** over and move the letters around and you can spell **nod**. **Nod** your head if you mean yes.
6. Change the first letter to spell **pod**. Peas grow in a **pod**.
7. Add 1 letter and you can spell **pods**. She shelled the peas from the **pods**.
8. Change the first letter and you will have **nods**. (NAME) **nods** her head to show she wants to come.
9. Let's spell one more 4-letter word, **pond**. I like to fish in a **pond**. Let's all stretch out **pond** and listen for the letters we need.
10. I bet you can get the secret word. (Add your last letter to **pond**, and what do you have? Yes. When you add **s** to **pond**, you have **ponds**.) There are lots of **ponds** near here.

Sort: Collect the letters, then read with the students all the words in the pocket chart. Next, have them sort the words into columns according to their first letter.

on	no	Don	so	pod
nod				pods
nods				pond
				ponds

Transfer: Say some words in sentences and have the students repeat the words and decide what letter they begin with.

odd	dig	purse	night	people	otter	doctor	soda

Word Wall: Call out the five words added to the Word Wall in Lesson 20—**pet, big, biggest, end,** and **rabbits**. Have the students chant them, write them, and check them. Remind them that the starred words will help them spell lots of rhyming words. Say the words **dig, bet, bend,** and **send**. Then, have students tell the words they rhyme with.

Lesson 22

Letters: e o d p p s t
Words: set pet pot dot top pop pest step stop stopped

Teach letter sounds: Before beginning to make words, have the students hold up each letter, name it, and say its common sound. Have the students show both the lowercase and capital letters.

Make words: Have the students make these words and send one student to make the word with the big letters. DO NOT wait for everyone to make the word before sending someone up. When the word is made with the big letters, ask everyone to check their words and fix them if necessary.

1. Take 3 letters and make **set**. It's time to **set** the table.
2. Change just the first letter and spell **pet**. I had a **pet** turtle.
3. Just change the vowel and you can spell **pot**. We cook spaghetti in a **pot**.
4. Change just the first letter to spell **dot**. Make a little **dot** next to your name.
5. Now, use 3 letters and spell **top**. I slept in the **top** bunk.
6. Change the first letter and spell **pop**. I like to watch popcorn **pop**.
7. Now, let's make a 4-letter word, **pest**. Sometimes, a little brother can be a **pest**. Let's all say **pest** and stretch it out so we can hear the letters we need.
8. Now let's do the "move the letters around" trick with **pest** to spell **step**. Be careful on that broken **step**.
9. Just change the vowel and you can spell **stop**. We have to **stop** at the **stop** sign.
10. Keep **stop** and add your remaining 3 letters to make the secret word. You have one minute to try to arrange all your letters to spell the secret word. The truck **stopped** to get gas. When you add **ed** to **stop**, you also need the other **p**.

Sort: Collect the letters, then read with the students all the words in the pocket chart. Next, have them sort the words into columns according to their first letter.

dot	pot	set	top
	pet	step	
	pop	stop	
	pest	stopped	

Transfer: Say some words in sentences and have the students repeat the words and decide what letter they begin with.

tooth saw page do puppy Sunday dinosaur table

Word Wall: Choose five words from the Word Wall for review. Have the students chant them, write them, and check them. Emphasize letter names, sounds, and formation as you do this each day.

© Carson-Dellosa CD-2409

Lesson 23

Letters: e o c k p s t
Words: set pet pot spot stop step sock peck speck pockets

Teach letter sounds: Before beginning to make words, have the students hold up each letter, name it, and say its common sound. Have the students hold up their **c** and **k** and tell them that they will need both the **c** and **k** to spell the **k** sound in some of the words.

Make words: Have the students make these words and send one student to make the word with the big letters. DO NOT wait for everyone to make the word before sending someone up. When the word is made with the big letters, ask everyone to check their words and fix them if necessary.

1. Take 3 letters and make **set**. <u>**Set** the table.</u>
2. Change the first letter to spell **pet**. <u>Do you have a **pet**?</u>
3. Change the vowel to spell **pot**. <u>We can plant flowers in a **pot**.</u>
4. Add a letter and you can spell **spot**. <u>I spilled juice and it made a big **spot** on the rug.</u>
5. Move the letters around and you can spell **stop**. <u>Please **stop** talking.</u>
6. Change the vowel and spell **step**. <u>**Step** up here.</u>
7. Now we are going to spell a 4-letter word and you will need the **c** and the **k** to spell that **k** sound. Take 4 letters and spell **sock**. <u>I can only find one **sock**.</u>
8. Let's use the **ck** again and spell **peck**. <u>Chickens **peck** at their food.</u>
9. Add 1 letter to **peck** and you can spell **speck**. <u>Please wipe every **speck** of crumbs off your desk.</u>
10. Now it's time for the secret word. It's a hard one and if no one gets it in a minute, I will give you some clues. (It starts with a **p**. You need your **ck** together in the middle. You can put keys and rocks and gum in them.) <u>You can put a lot of things in **pockets**.</u>

Sort: Collect the letters, then read with the students all the words in the pocket chart. Next, have them sort the words into columns according to their first letter.

set	pet
spot	pot
stop	pockets
step	peck
speck	
sock	

Transfer: Say some words in sentences and have the students repeat the words and decide what letter they begin with.

see pig park sandwich perfect Saturday

Word Wall: Choose five words from the Word Wall for review. Have the students chant them, write them, and check them. Emphasize letter names, sounds, and formation as you do this each day.

Lesson 24

Letters: a e n p r s t
Words: pen pan tan ten net nest rest pest past parents

Teach letter sounds: Before beginning to make words, have the students hold up each letter, name it, and say its common sound. Have the students show both the lowercase and capital letters.

Make words: Have the students make these words and send one student to make the word with the big letters. DO NOT wait for everyone to make the word before sending someone up. When the word is made with the big letters, ask everyone to check their words and fix them if necessary.

1. Let's start with a 3-letter word, **pen**. Can I borrow your **pen**?
2. Change the vowel and spell **pan**. Cook the eggs in a frying **pan**.
3. Change the first letter and spell **tan**. She drove a **tan** car.
4. Change the vowel again and spell **ten**. **Ten** is the number after nine.
5. Move the letters around and you can spell **net**. Shoot the ball into the **net**.
6. Add a letter and you can spell **nest**. The baby birds flew out of the **nest**. Let's all stretch out **nest** and listen for the letters we need.
7. Just change the first letter and you can spell **rest**. Who ate the **rest** of the pie?
8. Change the first letter again and spell **pest**. That mosquito is a **pest**.
9. Change the vowel and you can spell **past**. I walk **past** the post office on my way to school.
10. Now it's time for the secret word. It's a hard one, but try to use all your letters and spell one word. (It starts with a **p** and ends with an **s**. Many of you live with them.) Many students live with their **parents**.

Sort: Collect the letters, then read with the students all the words in the pocket chart. Next, have them sort the words into columns according to their first letter.

pen	tan	net	rest
pan	ten	nest	
parents			
pest			
past			

Transfer: Say some words in sentences and have the students repeat the words and decide what letter they begin with.

road neck paste top tornado nervous rescue pancakes

Word Wall: Choose five words from the Word Wall for review. Have the students chant them, write them, and check them. Say a word that rhymes with each of the starred words and have students decide the word it rhymes with.

Lesson 25
Word Wall Words: no on so stop stopped
Secret Words: ponds stopped pockets parents
Letters and Sounds for Review:
a (as in at); e (as in end); o (as in on); o (as in no); c d k n p r s t

To review the letters and sounds, the big letters for each secret word are put in the pocket chart and the students are invited to come and make words they remember from each lesson. (Students do not have their little individual letters.) Students should not try to make all the words from each lesson, but do have them make each secret word. Be sure they make the five words that will be added to the Word Wall.

Review

1. Put the big letters **o, d, n, p,** and **s** in the pocket chart. Let students come and make any words they can. If no one makes **on, no,** and **so,** ask someone to come and make them. Show them the Word Wall cards for **on, no,** and **so.**
2. Remove the **n** and add **e, t,** and **p**. Again, let students come and make some words. Be sure they make **stop** and **stopped** and show them the Word Wall cards for **stop** and **stopped**.
3. Remove the **p** and **d** and add **c** and **k**. Again, let students come and make some words.
4. Remove the **o, c,** and **k** and add **a, n,** and **r**. Again, let students come and make some words.

Word Wall

1. Place the words on the Word Wall. Have the students say each word and use each word in a sentence.
2. Help the the students notice that they have only one starred word, **stop**. Ask them to explain why **stop** has a star.
3. Point to each new word and have the students chant its spelling three times in a rhythmic manner ("**o-n, on; o-n, on; o-n, on**").
4. Have the the students write each new word as you model good writing on the board or overhead projector. Model and talk about correct letter formation as you write each word.
5. Have the students check their words by pointing to each letter and saying it aloud. Have them fix any words that need fixing.
6. If possible, give everyone a copy of the Take-Home Word Wall (page 162).

Lessons 26-30
Letters and Sounds: e (as in he); ch sh th

Lesson 26

Letters: i g h n s t
Words: in is his tin thin this sing sting thing things

Teach letter sounds: Before beginning to make words, have the students hold up each letter, name it, and say its common sound. Have the students hold up their **t** and **h** and tell them **t** and **h** together make a special sound. Have them say the words **the, this, that,** and **thing**, emphasizing the **th** sound.

Make words: Have the students make these words and send one student to make each word using the big letters. When the word is made with the big letters, ask everyone to check their words and fix them if necessary.

1. Take 2 letters and make the Word Wall word, **in**. We can all spell **in**.
2. Let's spell another Word Wall word, **is**. We can spell **is**, too.
3. Add a letter and you can spell **his**. This is **his** house.
4. Now, let's spell another 3-letter word, **tin**. Some houses have **tin** roofs.
5. Now, you are going to need your **th** to spell **thin**. Paper is very **thin**.
6. Change the last letter and spell **this**. I love **this** book.
7. You need 4 letters to spell **sing**. It is fun to **sing**.
8. Add 1 letter and you can spell **sting**. A bee can **sting** you.
9. Now change the first 2 letters and spell **thing.** What is that funny looking **thing**? Let's all say **thing** and stretch it out to hear all the letters.
10. I bet you can figure out the secret word. (Add your **s** and you will have it.) We have lots of **things** in our desks.

Sort: Collect the letters, then read with the students all the words in the pocket chart. Next, have them sort the words into columns according to their first letter, making a separate column for the **th** words.

in	his	tin	thin	sing
is			this	sting
			thing	
			things	

Transfer: Say some words in sentences and have the students repeat the words and decide what letter they begin with.

edge park door name donut sister enter nation

Word Wall: Call out the five words added to the Word Wall in lesson 25—**no, on, so, stop,** and **stopped**. Have the students chant them, write them, and check them. Say some rhyming words that the word **stop** will help them spell and have them repeat all the rhyming words after you: **stop, hop, mop, top, shop, chop, pop, drop,** and **flop.**

Lesson 27

Letters: e i c d h l n r
Words: Ed red rid lid led rich inch chin child children

Teach letter sounds: Before beginning to make these words, have the students hold up each letter, name it, and say its common sound. Have the students hold up their **c** and **h**, and tell them **c** and **h** together make a special sound. Have them say the words **chip, chin, child,** and **children.**

Make words: Have the students make these words and quickly send one student to make each word with the big letters. When the word is made with the big letters, ask everyone to check their words and fix them if necessary.

1. Take 2 letters and make **Ed**. Ed is late for school today. Do you remember what kind of letters names begin with?
2. Add a letter to make **red**. Some apples are red.
3. Change the vowel and you can spell **rid**. I finally got rid of my old car.
4. Change just the first letter to spell **lid**. Sometimes we call the cover we put on a pot a lid.
5. Change the vowel to spell **led**. (NAME) led the line to lunch.
6. Now, you will need your **ch** to spell a 4-letter word, **rich**. People who have a lot of money are rich.
7. You will need your **ch** again to spell another 4-letter word, **inch**. An inch is about this big. Stretch out **inch** and listen for the letters you need.
8. Do the "move the letters around" trick again and change **inch** to **chin**. Here is my chin.
9. Now let's spell a 5-letter word, **child**. The child was waiting for his father.
10. Add your remaining letters to the end of **child** and you can spell the secret word. (Give them a minute to try to figure it out and then say a sentence with the secret word.) You are all smart children!

Sort: Collect the letters, then read with the students all the words in the pocket chart. Next, have them sort the words into columns according to their first letter, making a separate column for the **ch** words.

red	Ed	inch	lid	chin
rid			led	child
rich				children

Transfer: Say some words in sentences and have the students repeat the words and decide what letter they begin with.

cheer	lunch	if	roar	energy	chocolate	raccoon	change

Word Wall: Choose five words from the Word Wall for review. Have the students chant them, write them, and check them. Emphasize letter names, sounds, and formation as you do this each day.

Lesson 28

Letters: e o d h p p s
Words: ho he she hop pop pep shed shop hopped shopped

Teach letter sounds: Before beginning to make words, have the students hold up each letter, name it, and say its common sound. When they hold up their **e**, tell them that sometimes **e** has the sound you hear in **he** and **she**. Have them say **he** and **she**. Have the students hold up their **s** and **h** and tell them **s** and **h** together make a special sound. Have them say the words **she, shed, shop,** and **shopped**, emphasizing the **sh** sound.

Make words: Have the students make these words and quickly send one student to make each word with the big letters. When the word is made with the big letters, ask everyone to check their words and fix them if necessary.

1. Take 2 letters and make **ho**. Santa says, "Ho, ho, ho."
2. Change the vowel and spell **he**. He is my friend.
3. Add a letter to **he** and you can spell **she**. She is my friend.
4. Let's spell another 3-letter word, **hop**. Rabbits **hop**.
5. Change just the first letter and make **pop**. It is fun to **pop** bubbles.
6. Just change the vowel and you can spell **pep**. When it is hot, my dog doesn't have much **pep**.
7. Now let's spell a 4-letter word **shed**. We keep our bikes in the **shed**.
8. Keep the **sh** and add 2 more letters and spell **shop**. I love to **shop**.
9. Now take 6 letters and spell **hopped**. The rabbits **hopped** down the road. You will need 2 **p's** in the middle just like our Word Wall word, **stopped**.
10. Add the last letter to **hopped** and you will have the secret word. I **shopped** at the mall yesterday.

Sort: Collect the letters, then read with the students all the words in the pocket chart. Next, have them sort the words into columns according to their first letter, including a separate **sh** column.

ho	pop	shed
he	pep	shop
hop		shopped
hopped		she

Transfer: Say some words in sentences and have the students repeat the words and decide what letter they begin with.

here   show   pan   ship   shower   power   holiday

Word Wall: Choose five words from the Word Wall for review. Have the students chant them, write them, and check them. Emphasize letter names, sounds, and formation as you do this each day.

Lesson 29

Letters: a i c d h n s w
Words: is his ash cash dash dish wish inch chin sandwich

Teach letter sounds: Before beginning to make words, have the students hold up each letter, name it, and say its common sound. Have the students hold up their **s** and **h** and say the words **she** and **shop**. Have them hold up their **c** and **h** and say the words **chin** and **children**.

Make words: Keep the lesson fast-paced. Send someone up quickly to make each word with the big letters. Remind the students to check each words and fix them if necessary.

1. Let's start with a 2-letter word, **is**. He **is** sick today.
2. Add a letter to spell **his**. **His** sister is sick today, too.
3. Now let's spell a 3-letter word, **ash**. When wood burns, it leaves **ash**.
4. Add a letter to spell **cash**. I need to **cash** a check.
5. Change the first letter to spell **dash**. I am going to **dash** into the store.
6. Change the vowel to spell **dish**. Here's a **dish** for your dessert.
7. Change the first letter to spell **wish**. Blow out the candles and make a **wish**.
8. Now start again and spell **inch**. The caterpillar was about an **inch** long.
9. Move the letters around to spell **chin**. I fell and bumped my **chin**.
10. Now it's time for the secret word. It's a hard one today because we have eight letters to use. In a minute, I will give you some clues. (Start your word with the **s**. Put the **ch** at the end. Some people make one with peanut butter and jelly.) I like a tomato **sandwich**.

Sort: Collect the letters, then read with the students all the words in the pocket chart. Next, have them sort the words into columns according to their first letter, including a separate **ch** column.

ash	inch	his	wish	cash	dash	chin	sandwich
is					dish		

Transfer: Say some words in sentences and have the students repeat the words and decide what letter they begin with.

help	down	chew	wet	it	at	children	cat

Word Wall: Choose five starred words from the Word Wall for review. Have the students chant them, write them, and check them. Say a word that rhymes with each of the starred words, and have students decide the word it rhymes with.

Lesson 30
Word Wall Words: children he she things this
Secret Words: things children shopped sandwich
Letters and Sounds for Review:
e (as in end); e (as in he); i (as in it);
a (as in at); o (as in on); o (as in no); sh; ch; th

To review the letters and sounds, the big letters for each secret word are put in the pocket chart and the students are invited to come and make words they remember from each lesson. (Students do not have their little individual letters.) Students should not try to make all the words from each lesson, but do have them make each secret word. Be sure they make the five words that will be added to the Word Wall.

Review

1. Put the letters **i, g, h, n, s,** and **t** in the pocket chart. Let the students come and make any words they can. If no one makes **things** and **this**, ask someone to come and make these words. Show them the Word Wall cards for **things** and **this.**
2. Remove the **g, s,** and **t** and add **c, d, e, l,** and **r**. Again, let students come and make words. Be sure they make **he** and **children** and show them the Word Wall cards for **he** and **children**.
3. Remove the **c, i, l, n,** and **r** and add **o, p, p,** and **s**. Again, let students come and make some words. Be sure they make **she** and show them the Word Wall card for **she**.
4. Remove the **e, p, p,** and **o** and add **a, i, c, n,** and **w**. Again, let students come and make some words.

Word Wall

1. Place the words on the Word Wall, have the students say each word, and use each word in a sentence.
2. Help the students notice that they have only one starred word, **things.** Tell them that the words **children, she, this,** and **things** will help them remember the sounds for **ch, sh,** and **th**.
3. Point to each new word and have the students chant its spelling three times in a rhythmic manner ("**s-h-e, she; s-h-e, she; s-h-e, she**").
4. Have the students write each new word as you model good writing on the board or overhead projector. Model and talk about correct letter formation as you write each word.
5. Have the students check their words by pointing to each letter and saying it aloud. Have them fix any words that need fixing.
6. If possible, give everyone a copy of the Take-Home Word Wall (page 163).

Lessons 31-35
Letters and Sounds: a-e (as in make)

Lesson 31

Letters: a e m n s
Words: me as an am Sam man mane same name names

Teach letter sounds: Tell the students that the vowel **a** can have the sound you hear in **at** and the sound in **ate**. Have the students practice both sounds for **a**. Have the students hold up their **e**. Tell them that in some of the words they will make today they won't hear any sound for the **e**, but it will be the letter that changes the sound of the **a**.

Make words: Keep the lesson fast-paced. Send someone up quickly to make each word with the big letters. Remind the students to check each word and fix it if necessary.

1. Take 2 letters and make **me**. <u>Please give **me** the book.</u>
2. Let's make another 2-letter word, **as**. <u>(NAME) is **as** tall **as** (NAME).</u>
3. Change the last letter and you can spell **an**. <u>I ate **an** apple.</u>
4. Change the last letter and spell the Word Wall word, **am**. <u>I **am** very happy.</u>
5. Add a letter and you can spell **Sam**. <u>I have a friend named **Sam**.</u>
6. Let's spell one more 3-letter word, **man**. <u>I saw a **man** walking down the road.</u>
7. Now we are going to change **man** to **mane** by adding that **e** that you won't hear. <u>I brushed the horse's **mane**.</u>
8. Let's spell another 4-letter word, **same**. <u>I always eat the **same** kind of ice cream.</u>
9. Change the first letter and you can spell **name**. <u>What is your **name**?</u>
10. I bet you can get the secret word. (Add your last letter to **name** and what do you have? When you add **s** to **name**, you have **names**.) <u>I have all your **names** on my list.</u>

Sort: Tell the students that today they are going to help you sort for rhyming words instead of beginning letters. Together with the students, read all the words they made. Then, take **am** and **Sam** and line them up. Have the students pronounce these words and notice that they rhyme. Do the same thing with **an/man** and **same/name**. Have the students pronounce all the rhymes with you and notice that the rhyming words have the same letters from the vowel to the end of the word. Tell them this is called the rhyming pattern. Let some students identify the rhyming patterns **am, an,** and **ame**.

am	an	same
Sam	man	name

Transfer: Tell the students that you want them to pretend they are reading and come to a word they don't know. They will use the rhyming words to help them figure it out. Show them the words **ham** and **came**, and have them put these words under the words with the same rhyming patterns. DO NOT allow anyone to pronounce the new words until they are lined up under the rhymes. Finally, have the students pronounce the new words by making them rhyme with the other words.

Word Wall: Call out the five words added in lesson 30—**children, he, she, things,** and **this**. Have the students chant them, write them, and check them. Remind students that **children, she, things,** and **this** will help them remember the sounds for **ch, sh,** and **th**. Say the following words and have them decide the two letters they begin with: **chop, shoe, thumb, chair,** and **ship**.

Lesson 32

Letters: a e k m r t
Words: at ate rat mat mate rate rake take make market

Teach letter sounds: Remind the students that the **a** can have the sound you hear in **at** and **ate** and that the **e** is often the letter that makes this change. You may want to tell them that some people call the **e** the "**magic e**" because of this.

Make words: Have the students make these words and send one student to make each word with the big letters. When the word is made with the big letters, ask everyone to check their words and fix them if necessary.

1. Take 2 letters and make the Word Wall word, **at**. Come to my house **at** 8:30.
2. Add the **e** and spell **ate**. (NAME) **ate** two cheeseburgers.
3. Use 3 letters and you can spell **rat**. The **rat** ran under the house.
4. Change the first letter to spell **mat**. Wipe your feet on the **mat**.
5. Now add a letter and change **mat** to **mate**. The bear is looking for a **mate**.
6. Change the first letter and spell **rate**. How would you **rate** that movie?
7. Change 1 letter and spell **rake**. I like to **rake** leaves.
8. Change the first letter and spell **take**. Please **take** this note home.
9. Change the first letter again and you can spell **make**. Let's **make** some cookies.
10. The secret word is tricky today. In just a minute, I will give you some clues. (Start with the **m**. Put the **t** at the end. This is a place where we buy things.) Let's go to the **market** and buy some groceries.

Sort: Tell the students that today they are going to sort for rhyming words. Have the students read with you all the words they made. Then, take **at** and **mat** and line them up, one above the other. Have the students pronounce these words and notice that they rhyme. Do the same thing with **ate/mate/rate** and **rake/ take/make**. Have the students pronounce all the rhymes with you and notice that the rhyming words have the same letters from the vowel to the end of the word. Tell them this is called the rhyming pattern. Let some students identify the rhyming patterns **at, ate,** and **ake**.

at	ate	rake
mat	mate	take
rat	rate	make

Transfer: Tell the students that they are going to pretend they are reading and come to a word they don't know. They will use the rhyming words to help them figure them out. Show them two words— **cake** and **date**—and have them put these words under the words with the same rhyming patterns. DO NOT allow anyone to pronounce these new words until they are lined up under the rhymes. Finally, have the students pronounce the new words by making them rhyme with the other words.

Word Wall: Choose five words from the Word Wall for review. Have the students chant them, write them, and check them.

Lesson 33

Letters: a e d r t
Words: Ed ad at ate red Ted rat rate date trade

Teach letter sounds: Remind the students that the **a** can have the sound you hear in **at** and **ate** and that the **e** is often the letter that makes this change. You may want to tell them that some people call the **e** the "**magic e**" because of this.

Make words: Keep the lesson fast-paced. Send someone up quickly to make each word with the big letters. Remind the students to check each word and fix it if necessary.

1. Take 2 letters and make **Ed**. <u>**Ed** ate all the cookies.</u>
2. Change the vowel to spell **ad**. <u>I found this car through an **ad** in the paper.</u>
3. Change the last letter to spell **at**. <u>We are **at** school.</u>
4. Add a letter and you can spell **ate**. <u>Who **ate** all the cereal?</u>
5. Start over and spell another 3-letter word, **red**. <u>Her car is bright **red**.</u>
6. Change the first letter and spell **Ted**. <u>**Ted** ate all the cereal.</u>
7. Let's spell one more 3-letter word, **rat**. <u>The **rat** ate all the cereal.</u>
8. Add a letter and spell **rate**. <u>How would you **rate** our team this year?</u>
9. Change the first letter and you can spell **date**. <u>What is today's **date**?</u>
10. Now it's time for the secret word. (Start with **tr** and put your **e** at the end.) <u>(NAME) likes to **trade** baseball cards.</u>

Sort: "We are going to sort for rhyming words again. Today, I want you to help me sort. I will take a word and you look for other words with the same rhyming pattern. I am taking **at**. Who can come and find another **at** word? Now, I am taking **red**, who can come and find two more **ed** words? Now, I am taking **date**. I need someone to come and find two more **ate** words." Have the students pronounce all the rhymes with you and notice that the rhyming words have the same letters from the vowel to the end of the word. Let some students identify the rhyming patterns **at, ed,** and **ate**.

at	red	date
rat	Ed	ate
	Ted	rate

Transfer: "Let's pretend we are reading and come to some words we don't know. We will use the rhyming words to help figure them out." Show them two words—**bed** and **gate**—and have them put these words under the words with the same rhyming patterns. DO NOT allow anyone to pronounce these new words until they are lined up under the rhymes. Finally, have the students pronounce the new words by making them rhyme with the other words.

Word Wall: Choose five words from the Word Wall for review. Have the students chant them, write them, and check them.

Lesson 34

Letters: a e k r s t
Words: as at ate rat rate Kate take takes skate skater

Teach letter sounds: Remind students how **e** at the end of a word changes the sound of **a**.

Make words: Keep the lesson fast-paced. Send someone up quickly to make each word with the big letters. Remind the students to check each words and fix them if necessary.

1. Let's start with a 2-letter word, **as**. He was **as** hungry **as** a bear.
2. Now spell **at**. **At** was one of our first Word Wall words.
3. Add a letter and spell **ate**. I **ate** breakfast this morning.
4. Let's spell one more 3-letter word, **rat**. Did you see that **rat**?
5. Add a letter and spell **rate**. How do you **rate** the movie?
6. Now let's spell a name, **Kate**. **Kate** is having a birthday.
7. Move the letters around and you can spell **take**. **Take** this pie to your grandma.
8. Add a letter and spell **takes**. It **takes** me 15 minutes to get to school.
9. Move the letters around and you can spell **skate**. I love to **skate**.
10. Now it's time for the secret word. (Add your remaining letter to **skate** and see if you can figure it out.) (NAME) is a wonderful **skater**.

Sort: "We are going to sort for rhyming words again. Today, I want you to help me sort. I will take a word and you look for other words with the same rhyming pattern. I am taking **at**. Who can come and find another **at** word? Now, I am taking **Kate**. Who can come and find three more **ate** words?" Have the students pronounce all the rhymes with you and notice that the rhyming words have the same letters from the vowel to the end of the word. Let some students identify the rhyming patterns **at** and **ate**.

at	Kate
rat	ate
	rate
	skate

Transfer: "Let's pretend we are reading and come to some words we don't know. We will use the rhyming words to help figure them out." Show them two words—**chat** and **that**—and have them put these words under the words with the same rhyming patterns. DO NOT allow anyone to pronounce these new words until they are lined up under the rhymes. Finally, have the students pronounce the new words by making them rhyme with the other words.

Word Wall: Choose five starred words from the Word Wall for review. Have the students chant them, write them, and check them. Say a word that rhymes with each of the starred words and have students decide which word it rhymes with.

© Carson-Dellosa CD-2409

Lesson 35
Word Wall Words: as make me same skate
Secret Words: names market trade skater
Letters and Sounds for Review: a (as in at); a-e (as in make)

To review the letters and sounds, the big letters for each secret word are put in the pocket chart and the students are invited to come and make words they remember from each lesson. (Students do not have their little individual letters.) Students should not try to make all the words from each lesson, but do have them make each secret word. Be sure they make the five words that will be added to the Word Wall.

Review

1. Put the big letters **a, e, m, n,** and **s** in the pocket chart. Let students come and make any words they can. If no one makes **as, me,** and **same,** ask someone to come and make these words. Show the students the Word Wall cards for **as, me,** and **same**.
2. Remove the **n** and **s**; add **k, r,** and **t**. Again, let students come and make some words. Be sure they make the word **make** and show them the Word Wall card for **make**.
3. Remove the **k** and **m**; add **d**. Again, let students come and make some words.
4. Remove the **d** and add **k** and **s**. Again, let students come and make words. If no one makes **skate**, ask someone to make it and show the class the Word Wall card for **skate**.

Word Wall

1. Place the words on the Word Wall, have the students say each word, and use each word in a sentence.
2. Help the students notice the stars on **make, same,** and **skate**. Get them to tell you why these words have stars (because they will help them spell lots of rhyming words).
3. Point to each new word and have the students chant its spelling three times in a rhythmic manner (**"o-n, on; o-n, on; o-n, on"**).
4. Have the students write each new word as you model good writing on the board or over-head projector. Model and talk about correct letter formation as you write each word.
5. Have the students check their words by pointing to each letter and saying it aloud. Have them fix any words that need fixing.
6. If possible, give everyone a copy of the Take-Home Word Wall (page 164).

Lessons 36-40
Letters and Sounds: i-e (as in ride); ight

Lesson 36

Letters: e i d p r s
Words: is Ed red rid rip ripe ride side pride spider

Teach letter sounds: Tell the students that the vowel **i** can have the sound you hear in **it** and also the sound in **ice** and **idea**. Have the students practice both sounds for **i**. Have the students hold up their **e**. Tell them that in some words they will make today they won't hear any sound for the **e**, but it will be the letter that changes the sound of the **i**.

Make words:

1. Take 2 letters and make the Word Wall word, **is**.
2. Let's spell a name we've spelled before, **Ed**.
3. Add a letter and you can spell **red**.
4. Change the vowel and you can spell **rid**. I want to get **rid** of these old games.
5. Change just the last letter to spell **rip**. I can **rip** this paper in half.
6. Add your **e** to **rip** and spell **ripe**. We pick berries when they are **ripe**.
7. Change 1 letter and spell **ride**. I like to **ride** horses.
8. Change 1 letter and you can spell **side**. Stand here on the left **side**.
9. Now let's spell a 5-letter word, **pride**. Everyone here takes **pride** in their work.
10. It's time for the secret word. I will give you one minute to see if anyone can get it. I saw a **spider** spinning a web.

Sort: "We are going to sort for rhyming words again. Today, I want you to help me sort. I will choose a word and you look for other words with the same rhyming pattern. I am taking **Ed**. Who can come and find another **ed** word? Now, I am taking **ride**. Who can come and find two more **ide** words?" Have the students pronounce all the rhyming words with you. Help them to notice that the rhyming words have the same letters from the vowel to the end of the word. Let some students identify the rhyming patterns **ed** and **ide**.

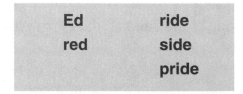

Ed	ride
red	side
	pride

Transfer: "Let's pretend we are reading and come to some words we don't know. We will use the rhyming words to help figure them out." Show the students two words—**led** and **hide**—and have them put these words under the words with the same rhyming patterns. DO NOT allow anyone to pronounce these two words until they are lined up under their rhyming words. Finally, have the students pronounce the new words by making them rhyme with the other words.

Word Wall: Call out the five words added in Lesson 35—**as, make, me, same,** and **skate**. Have the students chant them, write them, and check them. Say the words **bake, gate, came,** and **cake**. Then, have the students decide the words they rhyme with.

Lesson 37

Letters: e i b d r s
Words: be bed bid red rid ride rise side bride brides

Teach letter sounds: Remind the students that the **i** can have the sound you hear in **it** and **ice** and that the **e** is often the letter that makes this change. You may want to tell them that some people call the **e** the "**magic e**" because of this.

Make words:

1. Take 2 letters and make **be**. <u>I will **be** home at 3:30.</u>
2. Add a letter to make **bed**. <u>I made the **bed**.</u>
3. Change the vowel and you can spell **bid**. <u>I went to the auction and made a **bid**.</u>
4. Let's spell a word we've spelled many times before, **red**. <u>**Red** is my favorite color.</u>
5. Change the vowel to spell **rid**. <u>Let's clean out our desks and get **rid** of the trash.</u>
6. Add a letter to change **rid** into **ride**. <u>I like to **ride** on the train.</u>
7. Change just 1 letter and you can spell **rise**. <u>Every morning the sun will **rise**.</u>
8. Let's spell one more 4-letter word, **side**. <u>He was on my **side**.</u>
9. Now let's spell a 5-letter word, **bride**. <u>The **bride** was beautiful.</u>
10. Add your remaining letter to the end of **bride** and you can spell the secret word. I bet you can all figure it out. <u>**Brides** are happy on their wedding day.</u>

Sort: "Let's sort the rhyming words. We are looking for words with the same rhyming pattern. Who can go find some?" Have the students take the lead in finding the rhymes. Give them help as needed. Have them pronounce the rhyming words and identify the rhyming patterns **ed, id,** and **ide**.

red	rid	ride
bed	bid	side
		bride

Transfer: "Let's pretend we are reading and come to some words we don't know. We will use the rhyming words to help figure them out." Show the students two words—**did** and **wide**—and have them put these words under the words that have the same rhyming patterns. DO NOT allow anyone to pronounce these new words until they are lined up under the rhymes. Finally, have the students pronounce the new words by making them rhyme with the other words

Word Wall: Choose five words from the Word Wall for review. Have the students chant them, write them, and check them.

Lesson 38

Letters: e i d f n r s
Words: is in fin rid ride side dine fine friend friends

Teach letter sounds: Remind the students how **e** at the end of a word changes the sound of **i**.

Make words:

1. Take 2 letters and make the Word Wall word, **is**.
2. Let's spell another Word Wall word, **in**.
3. Add a letter and spell **fin**. A fish has **a fin**.
4. Let's spell another 3-letter word, **rid**. Get **rid** of the trash.
5. Change the first letter and make **ride**.
6. Change the first letter and you can spell **side**. Let's plant the tree on this **side** of the house.
7. Now let's spell another 4-letter word, **dine**. A fancy word for eat is **dine**.
8. Change the first letter and spell **fine**. Today is a **fine** day.
9. Now take 6 letters and spell **friend**. I like to go places with my **friend**. **Friend** is a tricky word because there is a letter you can't hear in a strange place.
10. Add the last letter to **friend** and you will have the secret word. I went camping with lots of my **friends**.

Sort: "Let's sort the rhyming words. We are looking for words with the same rhyming pattern. Who can go find some?" Have the students take the lead in finding the rhymes. Give them help as needed. Have the students pronounce the rhyming words and identify the rhyming patterns **in, ine,** and **ide**.

in	fine	ride
fin	dine	side

Transfer: "Let's pretend we are reading and come to some words we don't know. We will use the rhyming words to help figure them out." Show the students two words—**line** and **win**— and have them put these words under the words with the same rhyming patterns. DO NOT allow anyone to pronounce these new words until they are lined up under the rhymes. Finally, have the students pronounce the new words by making them rhyme with the other words.

Word Wall: Choose five words from the Word Wall for review. Have the students chant them, write them, and check them.

Lesson 39
Letters: e i f g h n r t
Words: fin fine fire hire tire night fight right fright frighten

Teach letter sounds: Tell the students that today they will make some words in which **i** has the sound you hear in **ice** and they will need the letters **igh** to spell that sound.

Make words: Keep the lesson fast-paced. Send someone up quickly to make each word with the big letters. Remind the students to check their words and fix them if necessary.

1. Let's start with a 3-letter word we have made before, **fin**. I saw the **fin** of the dolphin.
2. Add a letter to change **fin** to **fine**. The builders did a **fine** job.
3. Change 1 letter to spell **fire**. The house caught on **fire**.
4. Change the first letter to spell **hire**. I asked the boss to **hire** me to do the job.
5. Change the first letter again to spell **tire**. The car had a flat **tire**.
6. Now you will need to use **igh** to spell **night**. It gets dark at **night**.
7. Change the first letter to spell **fight**. The cats got into a **fight**.
8. Change the first letter again and spell **right**. You are **right**.
9. Add 1 letter to **right** to spell **fright**. The loud noise gave me a **fright**.
10. Now it's time for the secret word. Keep **fright** and add your remaining letters to it and see if you can figure out the secret word. I shouldn't let loud noises **frighten** me.

Sort: First, sort out the related words **fright** and **frighten** and have students use them in a sentence. Next, say to the students, "Let's sort the rhyming words. We are looking for words with the same rhyming pattern. Who can go find some?" Have the students take the lead in finding the rhymes. Give help as needed. Have the students pronounce the rhyming words and identify the rhyming patterns **ire** and **ight**.

fright		fire	right
frighten		hire	night
		tire	fight
			fright

Transfer: "Let's pretend we are reading and come to a word we don't know. We will use the rhyming words to help figure them out." Show the students the words **wire** and **light** and have them put these words under the words with the same rhyming patterns. DO NOT allow anyone to pronounce these new words until they are lined up under the rhymes. Finally, have the students pronounce the new words by making them rhyme with the other words

Word Wall: Choose five starred words from the Word Wall for review. Have the students chant them, write them, and check them. Say a word that rhymes with each of the starred words and have students decide the word it rhymes with.

Lesson 40

Word Wall Words: be friend night red ride
Secret Words: spider brides friends frighten
Letters and Sounds for Review: i-e (as in ride); ight

To review the letters and sounds, the big letters for each secret word are put in the pocket chart and the students are invited to come and make words they remember from each lesson. (Students do not have their little individual letters.) Students should not try to make all the words from each lesson, but do have them make each secret word. Be sure they make the five words that will be added to the Word Wall.

Review

1. Put the letters **i, e, d, p, r,** and **s** in the pocket chart. Let students come and make any words they can. If no one makes **red** and **ride,** ask someone to come and make these words. Show them the Word Wall cards for **red** and **ride.**
2. Remove the **p** and add **b.** Again, let students come and make some words. Be sure they make **be** and show them the Word Wall card for **be.**
3. Remove the **b** and add **f** and **n.** Again, let students come and make some words. Be sure they make **friend** and show them the Word Wall card for **friend**.
4. Remove the **d** and **s** and add **g, h,** and **t.** Again, let students come and make some words. Be sure they make **night** and show them the Word Wall card for **night**.

Word Wall

1. Place the words on the Word Wall, have the students say each word, and use each word in a sentence.
2. Help the students notice the stars on **night, red,** and **ride**.
3. Point to each new word and have the students chant its spelling three times in a rhythmic manner.
4. Have the students write each new word as you model good writing on the board or over-head projector. Model and talk about correct letter formation as you write each word.
5. Have the students check their words by pointing to each letter and saying it aloud. Have them fix any words that need fixing.
6. If possible, give everyone a copy of the Take-Home Word Wall (page 165).

Lesson 41

Letters: e o m n r s t
Words: to no not rot rose nose note notes stone monster

Teach letter sounds: Tell the students that the vowel **o** can have the sound you hear in **on** and also the sound in **old** and **over**. Have the students practice both sounds for **o**. Have the students hold up their **e**. Tell them that in some words they will make today they won't hear any sound for the **e**, but it will be the letter that changes the sound of the **o**.

Make words:

1. Take 2 letters and make **to**. We go **to** the library.
2. Let's make another 2-letter word, **no**. There are **no** cookies left.
3. Add a letter and you can spell **not**. He is **not** here today.
4. Change the first letter and you can spell **rot**. If these plants get too wet, they will **rot**.
5. Take 4 letters and use your **e** at the end to spell **rose**. He gave me a red **rose**.
6. Change the first letter and you can spell **nose**. You smell with your **nose**.
7. Change 1 letter in **nose** and you can spell **note**. Take this **note** home.
8. Add 1 letter to **note** and you can spell **notes**. She wrote me a lot of **notes**.
9. Move the letters around and you can spell **stone**. She threw a **stone** into the water.
10. It's time for the secret word, and it is a hard one. I will give you some clues if you need them. (Start your word with the **m**. Put the **r** at the end. This is a scary creature.) I had nightmares about the **monster** in the movie.

Sort: "Let's sort the rhyming words. We are looking for words with the same rhyming pattern. Who can go find some?" Have the students take the lead in finding the rhymes. Give them help as needed. Have the students pronounce the rhyming words and identify the rhyming patterns **ot** and **ose**.

not	rose
rot	nose

Transfer: "Let's pretend we are reading and come to a word we don't know. We will use the rhyming words to help figure the word out." Show them the words **shot** and **chose** and have them put these words under the words with the same rhyming patterns. DO NOT allow anyone to pronounce these new words until they are lined up under the rhymes. Finally, have the students pronounce the new words by making them rhyme with the other words.

Word Wall: Call out the five words added in lesson 40—**be, friend, night, red,** and **ride**. Have the students chant them, write them, and check them. Say some rhyming words—**bed, light, fed, side**— and have the students decide the words they rhyme with.

Lesson 42

Letters: e o b h r r s t
Words: hot rot Rob robe rose hose those other brother brothers

Teach letter sounds: Remind the students that the **o** can have the sound you hear in **on** and **old** and that the **e** is often the letter that makes this change. Some people call the **e** the "**magic e**" because of this.

Make words:

1. Take 3 letters and spell **hot**. <u>It is **hot** in here.</u>
2. Change the first letter and spell **rot**. <u>I hope these vegetables don't **rot**.</u>
3. Change the last letter and you can spell the name, **Rob**. <u>**Rob** likes to play basketball.</u>
4. Turn the capital **R** over, add a letter to **rob**, and spell **robe**. <u>The king wore a purple **robe**.</u>
5. Change 1 letter to spell **rose**. <u>A **rose** has thorns on its stem.</u>
6. Change the first letter and spell **hose**. <u>I use the **hose** to wash my car.</u>
7. Add 1 letter and spell **those**. <u>**Those** flowers are the prettiest.</u>
8. Let's spell one more 5-letter word, **other**. <u>Please come in the **other** door.</u> Let's stretch out **other** and listen for the letters we need.
9. Add 2 letters to the beginning of **other** and you can spell **brother**. <u>I have a little **brother**.</u>
10. I bet you can guess the secret word. (Add the **s** to **brother** and what do you have?) <u>My friend has three **brothers**.</u>

Sort: "Let's sort the rhyming words. We are looking for words with the same rhyming pattern. Who can go find some?" Have the students take the lead in finding the rhymes. Give them help as needed. Have the students pronounce the rhyming words and identify the rhyming patterns **ot, ose,** and **other**.

hot	rose	other
rot	hose	brother
	those	

Transfer: Tell the students that they are going to pretend they are reading and come to some words they don't know. They will use the rhyming words to help them figure these words out. Show them the words **mother** and **not**, and have them put these words under the words with the same rhyming patterns. DO NOT allow anyone to pronounce these new words until they are lined up under the rhymes. Finally, have the students pronounce the new words by making them rhyme with the other words.

Word Wall: Choose five words from the Word Wall for review. Have the students chant them, write them, and check them.

Lesson 43

Letters: e u d d h n r s
Words: us use Sue due end send dude rude under hundred hundreds

Teach letter sounds: Tell the students that the vowel **u** can have the sound you hear in **up**, and the sound in **use** and **uniform**. Have the students practice both sounds for **u**, then have them hold up their **e**. Tell them that in some words they will make today they won't hear any sound for the **e**, but it will be the letter that changes the sound of the **u**.

Make words:

1. Take 2 letters and make the Word Wall word, **us**.
2. Add the **e** to **us** to spell **use**. Can I **use** your crayons?
3. Turn the **s** over and move the letters around to spell the name **Sue**. Sue is my sister.
4. Change the first letter and you can spell **due**. The rent is **due** on the first of the month.
5. Let's spell another Word Wall word, **end**.
6. Add a letter and spell **send**. I will **send** a check for the rent.
7. Let's spell another 4-letter word, **dude**. He was a real cool **dude**.
8. Change the first letter and spell **rude**. It is **rude** to cut in line.
9. You need 5 letters to spell **under**. The book fell **under** the table. Let's stretch out **under** and listen for the letters we need.
10. Now you need seven letters to spell the word **hundred**. Ten tens make one **hundred**. Let's stretch out **hundred** and listen for the letters we need.
11. Now it's time for the secret word. (Add the **s** to **hundred** and what do you have?) We have **hundreds** of books in here.

Sort: "Let's sort the rhyming words. We are looking for words with the same rhyming pattern. Who can go find some?" Have the students take the lead in finding the rhymes. Give them help as needed. Have some students pronounce the rhyming words and identify the rhyming patterns **ue, end,** and **ude**.

Sue	end	dude
due	send	rude

Transfer: "Let's pretend we are reading and come to some words we don't know. We will use the rhyming words to help figure them out." Show students the words **bend** and **blue**, and have them put these words under the words with the same rhyming patterns. DO NOT allow anyone to pronounce these new words until they are lined up under the rhymes. Finally, have the students pronounce the new words by making them rhyme with the other words.

Word Wall: Choose five words from the Word Wall for review. Have the students chant them, write them, and check them.

Lesson 44

Letters: e o u c m m s t
Words: me to us use Sue cue cute mute commute commutes

Teach letter sounds: Remind the students that the **u** can have the sound you hear in **up** and **use** and that the **e** is often the letter that makes this change.

Make words: Have the students make these words and send one student to make the word with the big letters. DO NOT wait for everyone to make the word before sending someone up. Ask everyone to check their words and fix them if necessary.

1. Let's start with a Word Wall word, **me**.
2. Now spell **to**. Let's go **to** the mall.
3. Let's spell another Word Wall word, **us**.
4. Add a letter and spell **use**. Can I **use** your eraser?
5. Move the letters around and turn the lowercase **s** over to spell **Sue**.
6. Change the first letter and make **cue**. I will **cue** you when it is your turn to sing.
7. Add 1 letter and you can spell **cute**. Most new babies are **cute**.
8. Change the first letter and spell **mute**. Push the **mute** button on the TV.
9. Add 3 letters before **mute** and you can spell **commute**. Some people **commute** many miles to get to work.
10. Now it's time for the secret word. (Add your remaining letter to **commute** and see if you can figure it out.) My cousin **commutes** 100 miles each day.

Sort: "Let's sort the rhyming words. We are looking for words with the same rhyming pattern. Who can go find some?" Have the students take the lead in finding the rhymes. Give them help as needed. Have the students pronounce the rhyming words and identify the rhyming patterns **ue** and **ute**.

Sue	**cute**
cue	**mute**
	commute

Transfer: "Let's pretend we are reading and come to some words we don't know. We will use the rhyming words to help figure them out." Show students the words **true** and **flute**, and have them put these words under the words with the same rhyming patterns. DO NOT allow anyone to pronounce these new words until they are lined up under the rhymes. Finally, have the students pronounce the new words by making them rhyme with the other words.

Word Wall: Choose five starred words from the Word Wall for review. Have the students chant them, write them, and check them. Say a word that rhymes with each of the starred words, and have students decide which word it rhymes with.

Lesson 45

Word Wall Words: brother to those under use
Secret Words: monster brothers hundreds commutes
Letters and Sounds for Review: o-e (as in home); u-e (as in use)

To review the letters and sounds, the big letters for each secret word are put in the pocket chart and the students are invited to come and make words they remember from each lesson. (Students do not have their little individual letters.) Students should not try to make all the words from each lesson, but do have them make each secret word. Be sure they make the five words that will be added to the Word Wall.

Review

1. Put the big letters **e, o, m, n, r, s,** and **t** in the pocket chart. Let students come and make any words they can. If no one makes **to,** ask someone to come and make this word. Show them the Word Wall card for **to.**
2. Remove the **m** and **n** and add **b, h,** and **r.** Again, let students come and make some words. Be sure they make **those** and **brother** and show them the Word Wall cards for **those** and **brother.**
3. Remove the **o, b, r,** and **t** and add **u, d, d,** and **n.** Again, let students come and make some words. Be sure they make **under** and **use.** Show them the Word Wall cards for **under** and **use.**
4. Remove the **d, d, h, n,** and **r** and add **c, o, m, m,** and **t.** Again, let students come and make some words.

Word Wall

1. Place the words on the Word Wall, have the students say each word, and use each word in a sentence.
2. Help the students notice that **those** is the only starred word they have.
3. Point to each new word and have the students chant its spelling three times in a rhythmic manner.
4. Have the students write each new word as you model good writing on the board or overhead projector. Model and talk about correct letter formation as you write each word.
5. Have the students check their words by pointing to each letter and saying it aloud. Have them fix any words that need fixing.
6. If possible, give everyone a copy of the Take-Home Word Wall (page 166).

Lessons 46-50
Letters and Sounds: ay (as in day); ai (as in rain)

Lesson 46

Letters: a e l p r s y
Words: say Ray pay play pray spray relay replay player players

Teach letter sounds: Remind the students that the vowel **a** can have the sound you hear in **at** and **ate**. Have the students practice both sounds for **a**. Then, have them hold up their **y**. Tell the students that all the words they will make today will need **ay** to spell the **a** sound in **ate**.

Make words:

1. Take 3 letters and spell **say**. <u>What did you **say**?</u>
2. Change the first letter and spell the name **Ray**. <u>I have an Uncle **Ray**.</u>
3. Change the first letter again and spell **pay**. <u>I need to **pay** my bills.</u>
4. Add a letter and you can spell **play**. <u>My mother can **play** the piano.</u>
5. Change 1 letter to spell **pray**. <u>I **pray** it won't rain on Sunday.</u>
6. Add a letter to **pray** and spell **spray**. <u>I **spray** water with the hose when I wash my car.</u>
7. Lets spell another 5-letter word, **relay**. <u>Sometimes we run **relay** races.</u>
8. Add 1 letter to **relay** and you can spell **replay**. <u>Sometimes on TV, they show an instant **replay**.</u>
9. Move the letters around to spell **player**. <u>She was a great tennis **player**.</u> Let's stretch out **player** and listen for the letters we need.
10. It's time for the secret word. I bet you can all get it. <u>There are 5 **players** on a basketball team.</u>

Sort: All the words we made today had **ay** in them. Let's find the ones that end in **ay** and line them up and see if they all rhyme.

say	pray
Ray	spray
pay	relay
play	replay

Transfer: "Let's pretend we are reading and come to the words **stay** and **sway**." Have the students put **stay** and **sway** under the other words and pronounce all the **ay** words.

Word Wall: Call out the five words added in lesson 45—**brother, to, those, under,** and **use.** Have the students chant them, write them, and check them. Say the following words which rhyme with **those** and have the same spelling pattern. Then, have the students say these words after you: **those, nose, hose, rose, close, chose,** and **pose**.

Lesson 47

Letters: a a u d r s t y
Words: as at sat say day Ray tray stay stray Saturday

Teach letter sounds: Tell the students that today some of their words will need the **ay** to spell the sound of **a** in **ate**.

Make words:

1. Take 2 letters and make the Word Wall word, **as**.
2. Let's spell another Word Wall word, **at**.
3. Add 1 letter and you can spell **sat**. <u>I **sat** in the back of the airplane.</u>
4. Change just the last letter and spell **say**. <u>Did she **say** you could go?</u>
5. Change the first letter to spell **day**. <u>We are having a great **day**.</u>
6. Change a letter to spell the name **Ray** again.
7. Turn the capital **R** over, add 1 letter and you can spell **tray**. <u>I dropped my **tray** in the cafeteria.</u>
8. Let's spell one more 4-letter word, **stay**. <u>I hope I can **stay** overnight.</u>
9. Add 1 letter to **stay** and spell **stray**. <u>I found a **stray** dog.</u>
10. You need all your letters to spell the secret word. I will look and see if anyone has it, and then I will give you some clues. (It starts with an **s**—a capital **S.** It ends in **ay.** It is a name, but not a person's name.) **Saturday** <u>is my favorite day of the week.</u>

Sort: "Today we have two rhyming patterns for which to sort. Who can go and find some rhyming words?" Have the students sort and pronounce the **ay** and **at** words.

say	**at**
day	**sat**
Ray	
tray	
stay	
stray	
Saturday	

Transfer: Now it's "pretend-you're-reading-and-you-come-to-words-you-don't-know time." Show the students the words **hat** and **hay**, then have them put these words under the rhyming words and pronounce them.

Word Wall: Choose five words from the Word Wall for review. Have the students chant them, write them, and check them.

Lesson 48

Letters: a i n r s t
Words: I in an tan ran rain train stain strain trains

Teach letter sounds: Have the students hold up their two vowels and remind them of the sounds they have learned for these vowels. **I** has the sound you hear in **it** and **ice**. **A** has the sound you hear in **at** and **ate**. Today, some of the words will use **ai** to spell the sound of **a** in **ate**.

Make words:

1. Let's start with a word that has only 1 letter. You will need a capital letter to spell the word **I**. I see that you can all spell **I**.
2. Turn the **I** over and spell a Word Wall word, **in**.
3. Change the vowel and spell **an**. I would like to ride on **an** elephant.
4. Add a letter and spell **tan**. Tan is a light brown color.
5. Change the first letter and make **ran**. She was late and **ran** all the way home.
6. Add a letter and you can spell **rain**. I like to listen to the **rain**.
7. Add a letter to **rain** and spell **train**. I like to ride on the **train**.
8. Change the first 2 letters and spell **stain**. Ink will **stain** your clothes.
9. Today, there are 2 secret words. I will come around and see if anyone has them, and then I will give you some clues. (Many of you have **trains**. Move the **s** only and see what you can make.) Trains carry heavy things. Be careful when you pick up heavy things so you don't **strain** your back.

Sort: "Let's sort the rhyming words. We are looking for words with the same rhyming pattern. Who can go find some?" Have some students pronounce the rhyming words and identify the rhyming patterns **ain** and **an**.

rain	**an**
train	**tan**
stain	
strain	

Transfer: It's "pretend-you're-reading-and-you-come-to-words-you-don't-know time." Show the students the words **plan** and **chain**, then have them put these words under the rhyming words and pronounce them.

Word Wall: Choose five words from the Word Wall for review. Have the students chant them, write them, and check them.

Lesson 49

Letters: a e i n p r s t
Words: rain pain paint saint stain Spain train strain sprain painters

Teach letter sounds: Today we will need **ai** to make all our words.

Make words:

1. Let's start with a 4-letter word we have made before, **rain**.
2. Change the first letter to spell **pain**. Sometimes, I get a **pain** in my back.
3. Add 1 letter to **pain** to spell **paint**. (NAME) loves to **paint**.
4. Change the first letter to spell **saint**. Sometimes we call Santa Claus, **Saint** Nick.
5. Move the letters around and you can spell **stain**. I got a **stain** on my shirt.
6. Change 1 letter and you can spell the country of **Spain**. I would love to go to **Spain**. Did you remember to use a capital letter for a name?
7. Change the first 2 letters and spell **train**. The **train** goes fast.
8. Add a letter to **train** to spell **strain**. **Strain** was one of our secret words in the last lesson.
9. Change 1 letter to spell **sprain**. If you fall, you might **sprain** your ankle.
10. Now it's time for the secret word. It's a hard one, and I will give you some clues if you need them. (Begin the word with the **p**. Put **ers** at the end. These are people who **paint**.) The **painters** come tomorrow to paint the house.

Sort: First, sort out **paint** and **painters** and have the students notice that **painters** is **paint** with **ers** and that **painters** are people who **paint**. Next, have some students sort and pronounce the rhyming words and then identify the rhyming patterns **ain** and **aint**.

paint	rain paint
painters	pain saint
	stain
	Spain
	train
	strain
	sprain

Transfer: It's "pretend-you're-reading-and-you-come-to-words-you-don't-know time." Show the students the words **faint** and **brain**, then have them put these words under the rhyming words and pronounce them.

Word Wall: Choose five starred words from the Word Wall for review. Have the students chant them, write them, and check them. Say a word that rhymes with each of the starred words and have the students decide which word it rhymes with.

Lesson 50

Word Wall Words: day I player rain train
Secret Words: players Saturday trains painters
Letters and Sounds for Review: ay (as in day); ai (as in rain)

To review the letters and sounds, the big letters for each secret word are put in the pocket chart and the students are invited to come and make words they remember from each lesson. (Students do not have their little individual letters.) Students should not try to make all the words from each lesson, but do have them make each secret word. Be sure they make the five words that will be added to the Word Wall.

Review

1. Put the letters **a, e, l, p, r, s,** and **y** in the pocket chart. Let students come and make any words they can. If no one makes **player**, ask someone to come and make it. Show them the Word Wall card for **player.**
2. Remove the **e, l,** and **p** and add **a, u, d,** and **t.** Again, let students come and make some words. Be sure they make **day** and show them the Word Wall card for **day**.
3. Remove the **a, u, d,** and **y**; add **i** and **n**. Again, let students come and make some words. Be sure they make **I, rain,** and **train** and show them the Word Wall cards for **I, rain,** and **train**.
4. Add **p** and **e**. Again, let students come and make some words.

Word Wall

1. Place the words on the Word Wall, have the students say each word, and use each word in a sentence.
2. Help the students notice the stars on **day, rain,** and **train**. Point out that **rain** and **train** rhyme and have the same rhyming pattern.
3. Point to each new word and have the students chant its spelling three times in a rhythmic manner.
4. Have the students write each new word as you model good writing on the board or overhead projector. Model and talk about correct letter formation as you write each word.
5. Have the students check their words by pointing to each letter and saying it aloud. Have them fix any words that need fixing.
6. If possible, give everyone a copy of the Take-Home Word Wall (page 167).

Lessons 51-55
Letters and Sounds: ee (as in see); ea (as in eat)

Lesson 51

Letters: e e n p r s t
Words: see seep seen teen tree trees steer steep spree present

Teach letter sounds: Tell the students that the sound of **e** in **me** is often spelled with two **e's**. Ask them to hold up their two **e's** and tell them they will need to put these two **e's** together to spell many of today's words.

Make words:

1. Take 2 letters and make **see**. I **see** (NAME).
2. Add a letter to **see** and spell **seep**. The water will **seep** through the cracks.
3. Change the last letter and you can spell **seen**. Has anyone **seen** (NAME)?
4. Change the first letter and you can spell **teen**. When you are 13 to 19 years old, we call you a **teen**.
5. Let's spell one more 4-letter word, **tree**. The old **tree** was huge.
6. Add a letter and you can spell **trees**. **Trees** are fun to climb.
7. Move the letters in **trees** around and you can spell **steer**. You have to **steer** the car to stay on your side of the road.
8. Change the last letter and you can spell **steep**. We drove our car up a **steep** hill.
9. Remove the letter **t**, add another letter and you can spell **spree**. For my birthday, I went on a shopping **spree**.
10. It's time for the secret word, and it is a hard one. I will give you some clues if you need them. (Start your word with the **p**. Put the **s** in the middle and the **t** at the end. You might get one on your birthday.) I got the best birthday **present**.

Sort: "Let's sort the rhyming words. We are looking for words with the same rhyming pattern. Who can find some?" Have the children take the lead in finding the rhymes. Give them help as needed. Have the students pronounce the rhyming words and identify the rhyming patterns **ee, eep,** and **een**.

see	seep	seen
spree	steep	teen
tree		

Transfer: "Let's pretend we are reading and come to some words we don't know. We will use the rhyming words to help figure the words out." Show students the words **green** and **sheep**, then have them put these words under the words with the same rhyming patterns. DO NOT allow anyone to pronounce these new words until they are lined up under the rhymes. Finally, have the students pronounce the new words by making them rhyme with the other words.

Word Wall: Call out the five words added in lesson 50—**day, I, player, rain,** and **train**. Have the students chant them, write them, and check them. If there is time, call out the following words that rhyme with **day** or **rain/train** and have the students write these words: **pay, pain, play,** and **plain**.

Lesson 52

Teach letter sounds: Tell the students that they will need two **e**'s together to spell some of their words today.

Make words:

1. Take 2 letters and spell **ad**. <u>I put an **ad** in the paper to see if anyone had found my dog.</u>
2. Add a letter and spell **sad**. <u>I was so **sad** until I found my dog.</u>
3. Change the last letter and you can spell the word, **sap**. <u>**Sap** is sticky and comes from trees.</u>
4. Change the first letter to spell **cap**. <u>I got a new **cap** at the ball game.</u>
5. Now, use 3 letters to spell **see**. <u>I **see** you all remembered how to spell **see**.</u>
6. Add a letter and spell **seed**. <u>Plant the **seed** and cover it with soil.</u>
7. Change 1 letter and spell **seep**. <u>If it rains hard, water will **seep** under my door.</u>
8. Change just the first letter to spell **deep**. <u>Don't go in the **deep** part of the pool unless you can swim.</u>
9. Now, let's spell a 5-letter word, **speed**. <u>It is dangerous to **speed** down the road.</u>
10. The secret word today is a hard one. I will give you some clues. (Start it with **es** and put **ed** at the end. This is how the prisoner got out of jail.) <u>The prisoner **escaped** from the jail.</u>

Sort: "Let's sort the rhyming words. We are looking for words with the same rhyming pattern. Who can go find some?" Have the students take the lead in finding the rhymes. Give them help as needed. Have the students pronounce the rhyming words and identify the rhyming patterns **ad, ap, eed,** and **eep**.

ad	cap	speed	deep
sad	sap	seed	seep

Transfer: Tell the students that they are going to pretend they are reading and come to some words they don't know. They will use the rhyming words to help them figure these words out. Show them the words **need** and **sweep**, then have them put these words under the words with the same rhyming patterns. DO NOT allow anyone to pronounce these new words until they are lined up under the rhymes. Finally, have the students pronounce the new words by making them rhyme with the other words.

Word Wall: Teach word endings by choosing the Word Wall words **things, kittens, friend, brother,** and **train**. Have the students chant them, write them, and check them. Then, have them add **s** and write **friends, brothers,** and **trains**.

Lesson 53

Letters: a e u n p s t
Words: an at ate eat tea sea seat east neat peas peanuts

Teach letter sounds: Remind the students that the sound of **e** in **me** is often spelled with two **e**'s. Tell them that sometimes, **ea** together spell the sound of **e** in **me**.

Make words:

1. Take 2 letters and spell **an**. <u>Do you live in **an** old house?</u>
2. Let's quickly spell the Word Wall word, **at**.
3. Add a letter to **at** to spell **ate**. <u>We **ate** fried chicken at the picnic.</u>
4. Move the letters around and you can spell **eat**. <u>How much fried chicken did you **eat**?</u>
5. Move the letters again and spell **tea**. <u>We drank iced **tea**.</u>
6. Change the first letter and spell **sea**; not the **see** that you do with your eyes, but the **sea** that means ocean. <u>Fish swim in the **sea**.</u>
7. Add a letter and spell **seat**. <u>I saved that **seat** for you.</u>
8. Move the letters in **seat** around and spell **east**. <u>The sun comes up in the **east** and sets in the west.</u>
9. Take 4 letters and spell **neat**. <u>(NAME) has a **neat** desk.</u>
10. Now use 4 letters to spell **peas**. <u>I like corn and **peas**.</u>
11. Now it's time for the secret word. (It's something I like to eat. Keep the **pea** and move the **s** to the end.) <u>Elephants like **peanuts**, and so do I.</u>

Sort: "Let's sort the rhyming words. We are looking for words with the same rhyming pattern. Who can go find some?" Have the students take the lead in finding the rhymes. Give them help as needed. Have the students pronounce the rhyming words and then identify the rhyming patterns **ea** and **eat**.

eat	tea
seat	sea
neat	

Transfer: "Let's pretend we are reading and come to some words we don't know. We will use the rhyming words to help figure them out." Show students the words **cheat** and **heat**, then have them put these words under the words with the same rhyming patterns. DO NOT allow anyone to pronounce these new words until they are lined up under the rhymes. Finally, have the students pronounce the new words by making them rhyme with the other words.

Word Wall: Choose five words from the Word Wall for review. Have the students chant them, write them, and check them.

Lesson 54

Letters: a e e c h r t
Words: he the eat ear heat each reach teach cheat there teacher

Teach letter sounds: Remind the students that they will need **ea** to spell the **e** sound in **he** in some of their words.

Make words: Have the students make these words and send one student to make each word with the big letters. DO NOT wait for everyone to make the word before sending someone up. Ask everyone to check their words and fix them if necessary.

1. Let's start with a Word Wall word, **he**.
2. Add a letter to **he** to spell **the**. Let's go to **the** playground.
3. Use 3 letters to spell **eat**. When do we **eat**?
4. Change 1 letter and spell **ear**. Point to your **ear**.
5. Now let's spell a 4-letter word, **heat**. Let's turn up the **heat**.
6. Let's spell 1 more 4-letter word, **each**. Give two cookies to **each** person.
7. Add 1 letter and you can spell **reach**. Can you **reach** that book on the top shelf?
8. Change the first letter and spell **teach**. It is fun to **teach** you when you listen so well.
9. Move the letters in **teach** around and you can spell **cheat**. People don't like you when you **cheat** to win the game.
10. Take 5 letters and spell **there**. The ball rolled over **there**.
11. Now it's time for the secret word. (Start with **teach** and add the other letters.) I love being your **teacher**.

Sort: First, sort out the related words **teach** and **teacher**, and have the students use them in a sentence. Next, say to the students, "Let's sort the rhyming words. We are looking for words with the same rhyming pattern. Who can go find some?" Have the students take the lead in finding the rhymes. Give them help as needed. Have some students pronounce the rhyming words and identify the rhyming patterns **eat** and **each**.

teach
teacher

eat	reach
heat	each
cheat	teach

Transfer: "Let's pretend we are reading and come to some words we don't know. We will use the rhyming words to help figure them out." Show the students the words **beach** and **peach**, then have them put these words under the words with the same rhyming patterns. DO NOT allow anyone to pronounce these new words until they are lined up under the rhymes. Finally, have the students pronounce the new words by making them rhyme with the other words.

Word Wall: Choose five starred words from the Word Wall for review. Have the students chant them, write them, and check them. If there is time, call out a rhyming word for each starred word and have students write the rhyming word.

Lesson 55

Word Wall Words: an eat see the there
Secret Words: present escaped peanuts teacher
Letters and Sounds for Review: ee (as in see); ea (as in eat)

To review the letters and sounds, the big letters for each secret word are put in the pocket chart and the students are invited to come and make words they remember from each lesson. (Students do not have their little individual letters.) Students should not try to make all the words from each lesson, but do have them make each secret word. Be sure they make the five words that will be added to the Word Wall.

Review

1. Put the big letters **e, e, n, p, r, s,** and **t** in the pocket chart. Let students come and make any words they can. If no one makes **see,** ask someone to come and make it. Show them the Word Wall card for **see.**
2. Remove the **n, r,** and **t** and add **a, c,** and **d**. Again, let students come and make some words. Be sure they make **an** and show them the Word Wall card for **an.**
3. Remove the **e, c,** and **d** and add **u, n,** and **t**. Again, let students come and make some words. Be sure they make **eat** and show them the Word Wall card for **eat.**
4. Remove the **u, n, p,** and **s** and add **e, c, h,** and **r**. Again, let students come and make some words. Be sure they make **the** and **there** and show them the Word Wall cards for **the** and **there**.

Word Wall

1. Place the words on the Word Wall, have the students say each word, and use each word in a sentence. Be sure they notice that **an, eat,** and **see** have stars.
2. Point to each new word and have the students chant its spelling three times in a rhythmic manner ("**o-n, on; o-n, on; o-n, on**").
3. Have the students write each new word as you model good writing using the board or overhead. Model and talk about correct letter formation as you write each word.
4. Have the students check their words by pointing to each letter and saying it aloud. Have them fix any words that need fixing.
5. If possible, give everyone a copy of the Take-Home Word Wall (page 168).

Lesson 56

Letters: e i l l t t
Words: let lit lie tie ill till tell tile title little

Teach letter sounds: Have the students hold up their two vowels, and remind them of the sounds they have learned for these vowels. **I** has the sound you hear in **it** and **ice**. **E** has the sound you hear in **end** and **eat**. Today, some of the words will use **ie** to spell the sound of **i** in **ice**.

Make words:

1. Take 3 letters and spell **let**. Please **let** me see that book.
2. Change the vowel and spell **lit**. She **lit** a fire in the fireplace.
3. Take the **t** off and add a letter you can't hear to spell **lie**. You shouldn't tell a **lie**.
4. Change the first letter and spell **tie**. You can all **tie** your shoes.
5. Let's spell one more 3-letter word, **ill**. The old man was too **ill** to leave the house.
6. Add a letter and you can spell **till**. We **till** the garden before we plant.
7. Change the vowel and spell **tell**. I will **tell** you a story.
8. Take 4 letters and spell **tile**. I am having a new **tile** floor put in my kitchen.
9. Add 1 letter to **tile** and spell **title**. What is the **title** of your book? Let's stretch out **title** and see what letter we need to add and where to add it.
10. It's secret word time. In one minute, I will give you clues if you need them. (It begins with an **l**. It is the opposite of big.) The opposite of big is **little**.

Sort: Have the students pronounce all the words and sort them into rhyming patterns.

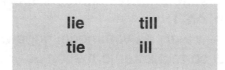

lie	till
tie	ill

Transfer: Show the students the two transfer words, **die** and **will**. Say to the students, "Let's pretend we are reading and come to these two new words." Have the students put the new words under the rhyming words and pronounce all the words.

Word Wall: Call out the five words added in lesson 55—**an, eat, see, the,** and **there**. Have the students chant them, write them, and check them. Have them decide which words rhyme with **beat, pan,** and **free** and use the patterns to spell these words.

Lesson 57

Letters: a o c r r s t
Words: to or at cat rat coat oats coats coast roast carrots

Teach letter sounds: Remind the students that the vowel **o** can have the sound you hear in **on** and **no.** Tell them that in some words, **oa** spells the **o** sound in **no.** Some of the words they will make today will need the **oa**, but they won't hear any sound for the **a**.

Make words:

1. Let's start with the Word Wall word, **to**.
2. Now spell another 2-letter word, **or**. <u>Do you want the red one **or** the green one?</u>
3. Let's do another Word Wall word, **at**.
4. Add a letter and you can spell **cat**.
5. Change just 1 letter to spell **rat**.
6. Now I want you to spell a 4-letter word, **coat**. <u>It is cold out and you need your **coat**.</u> Did you remember to use **oa**?
7. Let's spell another 4-letter word, **oats**. <u>Horses eat **oats**.</u>
8. Add 1 letter to **oats** and you can spell **coats**. <u>I have two **coats**.</u>
9. Move the letters in **coats** around and spell **coast**. <u>The **coast** is the land next to the ocean.</u>
10. Change the first letter again and spell **roast**. <u>I like to eat **roast** beef.</u>
11. It's time for the secret word. It's a hard one. I will give you a minute and then give you some clues. (It's a vegetable. It begins with a **c**. Rabbits like them.) <u>**Carrots** are good for you.</u>

Sort: Have the students pronounce all the words and sort them into rhyming patterns.

at	coats	coast
cat	oats	roast
rat		

Transfer: Show the students the two transfer words, **toast** and **boats**. Say to the students, "Let's pretend we are reading and come to these two new words." Have the students put the new words under the rhyming words and pronounce all the words.

Word Wall: Teach word endings by choosing the Word Wall words **things, kittens, see, skate** and **use**. Have the students chant them, write them, and check them. Then, have them add **s** and write **uses, sees,** and **skates**.

Lesson 58

Letters: a i o f g l n t
Words: at fat oil foil foal goal goat loan loaf float floating

Teach letter sounds: Tell the students that today some of their words will need the **oa** to spell the sound of **o** in **no**. They will also use the **oi** together to spell the sound they hear at the beginning of **oil**. Have everyone say **oil**.

Make words:

1. Take 2 letters and make the Word Wall word, **at**.
2. Add a letter to spell **fat**. That is a **fat**, little puppy.
3. Use 3 letters to spell **oil**. I need to have the **oil** changed in my car.
4. Add a letter and spell **foil**. Wrap that sandwich in **foil** and put it in the freezer.
5. Change just 1 letter to spell **foal**. A baby horse is called a **foal**.
6. Change the first letter to spell **goal**. My **goal** is to work very hard this year.
7. Change the last letter and you can spell **goat**. I petted the baby **goat**.
8. Let's spell another 4-letter word, **loan**. Can you **loan** me a dollar?
9. Change 1 letter and spell **loaf**. Go to the store and buy a **loaf** of bread.
10. Now, let's spell a 5-letter word, **float**. I can **float** and swim.
11. Keep **float** and add your remaining letters to spell the secret word. I bet you won't need clues today. I enjoy **floating** down the river on a raft.

Sort: First, sort out the related words **float** and **floating**, and have the students use them in a sentence. Then, have the students pronounce all the words and sort them into rhyming patterns.

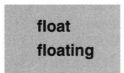

| float | | at | foil | foal | float |
| floating | | fat | oil | goal | goat |

Transfer: Show the students the two transfer words, **broil** and **throat**. Say to the students, "Let's pretend we are reading and come to these two new words." Have the students put the new words under the rhyming words and pronounce all the words.

Word Wall: Choose five words from the Word Wall for review. Have the students chant them, write them, and check them.

Lesson 59

Letters: e o d r s t y

Words: to so dot rot toy soy Roy Troy oyster destroy

Teach letter sounds: "Today we will need **oy** to spell some words that have the sound you hear in **boy** and **toy**." Have everyone say **boy** and **toy**.

Make words:

1. Let's start with a Word Wall word, **to**.
2. Change the first letter to spell **do**. <u>**Do** you like to make words?</u>
3. Add 1 letter to **do** to spell **dot**. <u>Put a **dot** next to every word you spelled correctly.</u>
4. Change the first letter to spell **rot**. <u>If you leave vegetables out too long, they **rot**.</u>
5. Use 3 letters to spell **toy**. <u>I got a **toy** car for my birthday.</u>
6. Change just 1 letter and you can spell **soy**. <u>When I eat Chinese food, I like **soy** sauce.</u>
7. Change the first letter and spell **Roy**. <u>**Roy** is my neighbor.</u>
8. Turn the capital **R** over and add a letter to **roy** to spell **Troy**. <u>**Troy** is Roy's twin brother.</u>
9. The next word takes 6 letters, **oyster**. <u>I like to eat **oyster** stew.</u> Let's stretch out **oyster** and listen for the letters we need.
10. Now it's time for the secret word. It's a hard one, and if I need to, I will give you some clues. (Begin the word with the **d**. Put **oy** at the end. A tornado can do this to buildings.) <u>A tornado can **destroy** all the buildings in its path.</u>

Sort: Have the students pronounce all the words and sort them into rhyming patterns.

to	dot	toy
do	rot	soy
		Roy
		Troy
		destroy

Transfer: Show the students the two transfer words, **boy** and **spot**. Say to the students, "Let's pretend we are reading and come to these two new words." Have the students put the new words under the rhyming words and pronounce all the words.

Word Wall: Choose five starred words from the Word Wall for review. Have the students chant them, write them, and check them. If there is time, call out a few words that rhyme with and have the same pattern as the Word Wall word, then have the students spell these words.

Lesson 60

Word Wall Words: float oil or little tell
Secret Words: little carrots floating destroy
Letters and Sounds for Review: oa (as in coat); ie (as in lie); oi; oy

To review the letters and sounds, the big letters for each secret word are put in the pocket chart and the students are invited to come and make words they remember from each lesson. (Students do not have their little individual letters.) Students should not try to make all the words from each lesson, but do have them make each secret word. Be sure they make the five words that will be added to the Word Wall.

Review

1. Put the letters **e, i, l, l, t,** and **t** in the pocket chart. Let students come and make any words they can. If no one makes **tell** and **little,** ask someone to come and make them. Show them the Word Wall cards for **tell** and **little.**
2. Remove all the letters except for 1 **t.** Add **a, o, c, r, r,** and **s.** Again, let students come and make some words. Be sure they make **or** and show them the Word Wall card for **or.**
3. Remove all the letters except **a, o,** and **t.** Add **i, f, g, l,** and **n.** Again, let students come and make some words. Be sure they make **floating** and **oil** and show them the Word Wall cards for **floating** and **oil.**
4. Remove all the letters except **o** and **t.** Add the **e, d, r, s,** and **y.** Again, let students come and make some words.

Word Wall

1. Place the words on the wall, have the students say each word, and use each word in a sentence. Be sure the students notice that **float, oil,** and **tell** have stars.
2. Point to each new word and have the students chant its spelling three times in a rhythmic manner.
3. Have the students write each new word as you model good writing using the board or overhead. Model and talk about correct letter formation as you write each word.
4. Have the students check their words by pointing to each letter and saying it aloud. Have them fix any words that need fixing.
5. If possible, give everyone a copy of the Take-Home Word Wall (page 169).

Lessons 61-65
Letters and Sounds: ar; or

Lesson 61

Letters: a m r s t
Words: at sat rat tar art arm arms Mars star smart

Teach letter sounds: Tell the students that the letters **ar** together often make the sound you hear in **car**. Have the students hold up their **ar** and make this sound.

Make words:

1. Take 2 letters and make **at**.
2. Add a letter and spell **sat**. She **sat** on the sofa.
3. Change the first letter and you can spell **rat**.
4. Move the letters in **rat** and you can spell **tar**. Some roads are paved with **tar**.
5. Move the letters again and spell **art**. We love to go to **art** class.
6. Change 1 letter and you can spell **arm**. I broke my right **arm**.
7. Add 1 letter and you can spell **arms**. I was glad I didn't break both **arms**.
8. Move the letters and you can spell **Mars**. **Mars** is one of the planets. Did you remember to use your capital **M** for a name?
9. Let's spell one more 4-letter word, **star**. I saw a very bright **star** in the sky.
10. It's time for the secret word, and I bet you can figure it out because it's what you are! You are very **smart**.

Sort: Have the students pronounce all the words and sort them into rhyming patterns.

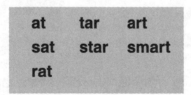

at	tar	art
sat	star	smart
rat		

Transfer: Show the students the two transfer words, **car** and **chart**. Say to the students, "Let's pretend we are reading and come to these two new words." Have the students put the new words under the rhyming words and pronounce all the words.

Word Wall: Call out the five words added in lesson 60—**float, oil, or, little,** and **tell**. Have the students chant them, write them, and check them. Call out a few words (**boil, boat, bell,** and **spell**) that rhyme with **float, oil,** or **tell** and have the students write the four new words.

Lesson 62

Letters: a e c d n r s
Words: an can car cars scar care dare scare scared dancers

Make Words:

1. Take 2 letters and spell the Word Wall word, **an**.
2. Add a letter and spell another Word Wall word, **can**.
3. Change the last letter and spell a word we are going to add to the Word Wall, **car**.
4. Add a letter to spell **cars**.
5. Move the letters in **cars** to spell **scar**. I have a **scar** from a cut I got when I was very little.
6. Make **car** again and add a letter to spell **care**. (NAME) takes **care** of his little sister.
7. Change just 1 letter and spell **dare**. I **dare** you to run all the way to the end of the field.
8. Now let's spell a 5-letter word, **scare**. You can't **scare** me with those silly stories.
9. Add a letter to **scare** and you will have **scared**. (Name) isn't **scared** of anything!
10. The secret word today is a hard one. I will wait one minute and then give you some clues. (Start it with the **d** and put **s** at the end. The **c** goes in the middle and has an **s** sound instead of its usual **k** sound.) I loved watching the **dancers** on the stage.

Sort: First, sort out the related words **scare** and **scared**, and have students use them in a sentence. Then, have the students pronounce all the words and sort them into rhyming patterns. Have the students pronounce the rhymes and notice the different sounds of **a, ar,** and **are**.

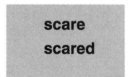

scare
scared

an	car	scare
can	scar	care
		dare

Transfer: Show the students the two transfer words, **stare** and **star**. Say to the students, "Let's pretend we are reading and come to these two new words." Have the students put the new words under the rhyming words and pronounce all the words.

Word Wall: Teach word endings by choosing **stop, stopped, jump, rain,** and **skate**. Have the students chant them, write them, and check them. Then, have the students add **ed** and write **jumped, rained,** and **skated**. Tell them that sometimes spelling changes a little when we add endings. The **p** in **stop** is doubled when we add **ed.** When a word ends in **e** like **skate,** we just add the **d.**

Lesson 63

Letters: e o f r s t
Words: so of or for fort sort sore tore store forest

Teach letter sounds: Tell the students that the letters **or** together often make the sound you hear in **for**. Have the students hold up their **or** and make this sound.

Make words:

1. Take 2 letters and spell the Word Wall word, **so.**

2. Now we're going to use 2 letters and spell a word that isn't spelled the way it sounds. See if you can figure out how to spell **of**. I had a big piece **of** apple pie.

3. Change 1 letter to spell **or**. Do you want a baked potato **or** French fries?

4. Add a letter and you can spell **for**. I brought snacks **for** you.

5. Add another letter and spell **fort**. Let's build a **fort.**

6. Change the first letter and spell **sort**. Every day, we **sort** the words into rhyming patterns.

7. Change a letter and spell **sore**. I had a **sore** throat.

8. Change the first letter and spell **tore**. He got mad and **tore** up the paper.

9. Add a letter to **tore** and spell **store**. Let's go to the **store.**

10. Now it's time for the secret word. (It's a place with lots of trees where animals live. It begins with an **f** and ends with a **t**.) There are lots of trees and animals in the **forest.**

Sort: Have the students pronounce all the words and sort them into rhyming patterns. Help them notice that the rhyming patterns **or** and **ore** have the same pronunciation.

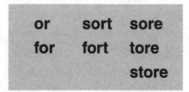

or	sort	sore
for	fort	tore
		store

Transfer: Show the students the two transfer words, **short** and **sport**. Say to the students, "Let's pretend we are reading and come to these two new words." Have the students put the new words under the rhyming words and pronounce all the words.

Word Wall: Choose five **th** words from the Word Wall—**things, this, there, the,** and **those**. Have the students chant them, write them, and check them. Talk about the sound of **th** and have the students say some sentences with these easily confused words.

Lesson 64

Letters: a o p r r s t
Words: or at rat art tar star part port sort sport parrots

Teach letter sounds: In this lesson, we are going to spell some **ar** words and some **or** words.

Make words: Have the students make these words and send one student to make each word using the big letters. DO NOT wait for everyone to make the word before sending someone up. Ask everyone to check their words and fix them if necessary.

1. Let's start with a 2-letter word, **or**. I don't know whether to drive **or** walk.
2. Now let's spell **at**.
3. Add a letter to spell **rat**.
4. Move the letters and spell **art**. I made this in **art** class.
5. Move the letters again and spell **tar**. My shoes had **tar** on them from walking on the hot road.
6. Add 1 letter to spell **star**. Make a wish on the first **star**.
7. Let's spell another 4-letter word, **part**. He got a good **part** in the play.
8. Change the vowel and spell **port**. Ships dock at the **port**.
9. Change the first letter and you can spell **sort**. **Sort** the blocks by color.
10. Add 1 letter and spell **sport**. My favorite **sport** is basketball.
11. Now it's time for the secret word. (It starts with a **p** and ends with **s**. These birds can learn to talk.) **Parrots** are birds that can learn to talk.

Sort: Have the students pronounce all the words and sort them into rhyming patterns.

at	part	tar	port
rat	art	star	sort
			sport

Transfer: Show the students the two transfer words, **fort** and **start**. Say to the students, "Let's pretend we are reading and come to these two new words." Have the students put the new words under the rhyming words and pronounce all the words.

Word Wall: Choose five starred words from the Word Wall for review. Have the students chant them, write them, and check them. Say a few words that rhyme with and have the same pattern as the Word Wall words, and have the students spell these new words.

Lesson 65
Word Wall Words: car for of smart sport
Secret Words: smart dancers forest parrots
Letters and Sounds for Review: ar; or

To review the letters and sounds, the big letters for each secret word are put in the pocket chart and the students are invited to come and make words they remember from each lesson. (Students do not have their little individual letters.) Students should not try to make all the words from each lesson, but do have them make each secret word. Be sure they make the five words that will be added to the Word Wall.

Review:

1. Put the big letters **a, m, r, s,** and **t** in the pocket chart. Let students come and make any words they can. If no one makes **smart**, ask someone to come and make it. Show them the Word Wall card for **smart**.

2. Remove the **m** and **t** and add **e, c, d,** and **n**. Again, let students come and make some words. If no one makes **car**, ask someone to come and make it. Show them the Word Wall card for **car**.

3. Remove the **a, c, d,** and **n** and add **o, f,** and **t**. Again, let students come and make some words. Be sure they make **of** and **for** and show them the Word Wall cards for **of** and **for**.

4. Remove the **e** and **f** and add **a, p,** and **r**. Again, let students come and make some words. Be sure they make **sport** and show them the Word Wall card for **sport**.

Word Wall:

1. Place the words on the Word Wall, have the students say each word, and use each word in a sentence. Be sure the students notice that **car, smart,** and **sport** have stars.

2. Point to each new word and have the students chant its spelling three times in a rhythmic manner ("**o-n, on; o-n, on; o-n, on**").

3. Have the students write each new word as you model good writing using the board or overhead. Model and talk about correct letter formation as you write each word.

4. Have the students check their words by pointing to each letter and saying it aloud. Have them fix any words that need fixing.

5. If possible, give everyone a copy of the Take-Home Word Wall (page 170).

Lessons 66-70
Letters and Sounds: er; ir; ur

Lesson 66

Letters: i f r s t
Words: if it sit fit fir sir stir fits fist first

Teach letter sounds: Have the students hold up their **i** and **r**. Tell them that some of the words they will make today will have the **ir** sound they hear in **girl**. Have them make that sound.

Make words: Have the students make these words and send one student to make the word with the big letters. Ask everyone to check their words and fix them if necessary.

1. Let's start with a Word Wall word, **if**.
2. Now spell another Word Wall word, **it**.
3. Add a letter to spell **sit**.
4. Change the first letter and spell **fit**. These shoes do not **fit** anymore.
5. Change 1 letter and spell **fir**. A **fir** tree stays green all year.
6. Change a letter and you can spell **sir**. People in the army call their officers **sir**.
7. Add a letter and spell **stir**. **Stir** the soup so it doesn't stick to the pan.
8. Take 4 letters and spell **fits**. This jacket **fits** fine.
9. Move the letters around and spell **fist**. Make a **fist** with your hand.
10. It's secret word time. Add the **r** somewhere in **fist** and see what you have. Everyone likes to be **first** in line.

Sort: Have the students pronounce all the words and sort them into rhyming patterns.

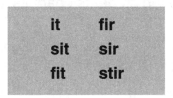

it	fir
sit	sir
fit	stir

Transfer: Show the students the two transfer words, **bit** and **hit**. Say to the students, "Let's pretend we are reading and come to these two new words." Have the students put the new words under the rhyming words and pronounce all the words.

Word Wall: Call out the five words added in lesson 65—**car, for, of, smart,** and **sport**. Have the students chant them, write them, and check them. Call out the following rhyming words and have the students spell them: **short, chart, star,** and **Bart**.

Lesson 67

Letters: a e f h r s t
Words: he her she far tar star fast raft after faster fathers

Teach letter sounds: Have the students hold up their **e** and **r**. Tell them that some of the words they will make today will have the **er** sound they hear in **her**. Have them make that sound. Tell them that this is the same sound that they spelled yesterday with the **ir**, and that it can be spelled with both the **ir** and the **er**.

Make words:

1. Let's start with the Word Wall word, **he**.
2. Add a letter and spell **her**. <u>I saw **her** walking to school.</u>
3. Let's do another Word Wall word, **she**.
4. Take 3 letters and spell **far**. <u>Do you live **far** from here?</u>
5. Change just 1 letter to spell **tar**.
6. Add a letter to spell **star**.
7. Let's spell another 4-letter word, **fast**. <u>(NAME) can run **fast**.</u>
8. Start again and use 4 letters to spell **raft**. <u>I went down the river on a **raft**.</u>
9. Now let's spell a 5-letter word, **after**. <u>**After** school, I am going shopping.</u> Let's all stretch out **after** and listen for the letters we need.
10. Take six letters and spell **faster**. <u>My dog can run **faster** than I can.</u>
11. It's time for the secret word. I will give you a minute, and then give you some clues. (It begins with a **f** and ends with **s**. Put the **th** in the middle. Sometimes we call them dads.) <u>We went to the ball game with our **fathers**.</u>

Sort: First, have the students sort out **fast** and **faster**. Help them notice that **faster** is **fast** with **er** and that someone who can run **faster** is a better runner than someone who runs **fast**. Next, have the students sort all the words into rhyming patterns.

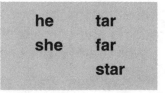

Transfer: Show the students the two transfer words, **scar** and **jar**. Say to the students, "Let's pretend we are reading and come to these two new words." Have the students put the new words under the rhyming words and pronounce all the words.

Word Wall: Teach endings by choosing **jump, jumping, float, rain,** and **skate**. Have the students chant them, write them, and check them. Then, have them add **ing** and write **floating, raining,** and **skating**. Tell them that sometimes spelling changes a little when we add endings. When a word ends in **e** like **skate**, we drop the **e** and add **ing**.

Lesson 68

Letters: e o h m r s t
Words: he her more sore some sort short store other mother smother mothers

Teach letter sounds: Tell the students that today some of their words will need the **or** they hear in **for** and some words will need the **er** they hear in **her**.

Make words:

1. Take 2 letters and make the Word Wall word, **he**.
2. Add a letter to spell **her**. Today is **her** birthday.
3. Use 4 letters to spell **more**. Could I please have some **more** ice cream?
4. Change a letter and spell **sore**. My arm was **sore** after I broke it.
5. Change just 1 letter to spell **some**. **Some** people like chocolate ice cream best.
6. Let's spell 1 more 4-letter word, **sort**. After we make words, we **sort** them.
7. Add a letter and you can spell **short**. Some people are tall and some are **short**.
8. Use 5 letters to spell **store**.
9. Let's spell one more 5-letter word, **other**. We have to go out the **other** door because this one is broken. Let's all stretch out **other** and listen for the letters we need.
10. Add 1 letter to **other** and you will have **mother**. Ask your **mother** if you can go.
11. Today we have two secret words. Put your **s** on both ends of **mother** and see what you get. We made gifts for our **mothers**. Be careful you don't **smother** the baby.

Sort: Have the students pronounce all the words and sort them into rhyming patterns.

more	sort	other
sore	short	mother
store		smother

Transfer: Show the students the two transfer words, **core** and **shore**. Say to the students, "Let's pretend we are reading and come to these two new words." Have the students put the new words under the rhyming words and pronounce all the words.

Word Wall: Call out **day, rain, train, skate,** and **make**. Have the students chant, write, and check them. Help them to notice the sound of **a** in all the words and how that sound is spelled—**ay, ai,** or **a-e**.

Lesson 69

Letters: i u g h n r t

Words: hug rug run nut hut hunt hurt turn grunt hurting

Teach letter sounds: Have the students hold up their **u** and **r**. Tell them that some of the words they will make today will have the **ur** sound they hear in **hurt**. Have them make that sound. Tell them that this is the same sound that they spelled with the **ir** and the **er**.

Make words:

1. Let's start with a 3-letter word, **hug**. <u>Give your grandma a **hug**.</u>
2. Change the first letter to spell **rug**. <u>Please come sit on the **rug**.</u>
3. Change the last letter to spell **run**. <u>We all like to **run**.</u>
4. Use 3 letters to spell **nut**. <u>The squirrel was eating the **nut**.</u>
5. Change 1 letter to spell **hut**. <u>We built a **hut** to play in.</u>
6. Add 1 letter and you can spell **hunt**. <u>Do you like to **hunt**</u>?
7. Change 1 letter and spell **hurt**. <u>I fell and **hurt** my leg.</u>
8. Start over and spell another 4-letter word, **turn**. <u>It's my **turn** to swing.</u>
9. The next word takes 5 letters—**grunt**. <u>Did you hear that loud **grunt**?</u>
10. Now it's time for the secret word. I bet someone will get it today. (Begin the word **hurt** and add all the letters to it.) <u>My head has been **hurting** all morning.</u>

Sort: First, sort out the related words **hurt** and **hurting**, and have students use them in a sentence. Then, have the students pronounce all the words and sort them into rhyming patterns.

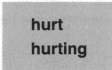

hug	nut	hunt
rug	hut	grunt

Transfer: Show the students the two transfer words, **shut** and **plug**. Say to the students, "Let's pretend we are reading and come to these two new words." Have the students put the new words under the rhyming words and pronounce all the words.

Word Wall: Choose five starred words from the Word Wall for review. Have the students chant them, write them, and check them. Say a few words that rhyme with and have the same pattern as the Word Wall word and have the students spell these new words.

Lesson 70

Word Wall Words: after her hurt more some
Secret Words: first fathers mothers smother hurting
Letters and Sounds for Review: er; ir; ur

To review the letters and sounds, the big letters for each secret word are put in the pocket chart and the students are invited to come and make words they remember from each lesson. (Students do not have their little individual letters.) Students should not try to make all the words from each lesson, but do have them make each secret word. Be sure they make the five words that will be added to the Word Wall.

Review:

1. Put the letters **i, f, r, s,** and **t** in the pocket chart. Let students come and make any words they can.

2. Remove the **i**. Add **a, e,** and **h**. Again, let students come and make some words. Be sure they make **after** and **her** and show them the Word Wall cards for **after** and **her**.

3. Remove the **a** and **f**. Add **o** and **m**. Again, let students come and make some words. Be sure they make **more** and **some** and show them the Word Wall cards for **more** and **some**.

4. Remove the **e, o, m,** and **s**. Add the **i, u, g,** and **n**. Again, let students come and make some words. Be sure they make **hurt** and show them the Word Wall card for **hurt**.

Word Wall:

1. Place the words on the Word Wall, have the students say each word, and use each word in a sentence. Be sure they notice that **more** is the only word with a star.

2. Point to each new word and have the students chant its spelling three times in a rhythmic manner.

3. Have the students write each new word as you model good writing using the board or overhead. Model and talk about correct letter formation as you write each word.

4. Have the students check their words by pointing to each letter and saying it aloud. Have them fix any words that need fixing.

5. If possible, give everyone a copy of the Take-Home Word Wall (page 171).

Lessons 71-75
Letters and Sounds: aw; au; al

Lesson 71

Letters: a c l r s w
Words: as was saw raw law claw slaw cars scar crawl crawls

Teach letter sounds: Tell the students that the letters **aw** together often make the sound you hear in **saw**. Have the students hold up their **aw** and make this sound.

Make words:

1. Take 3 letters and make the Word Wall word, **car**.
2. Let's spell another 3-letter word, **was**. I **was** here early this morning.
3. Move the letters around and you can spell **saw**. I **saw** (NAME) coming to school.
4. Change 1 letter and you can spell **raw**. I like **raw** carrots.
5. Change 1 letter and spell **law**. We all have to follow the **law**.
6. Add 1 letter and you can spell **claw**. A crab has a **claw**.
7. Change 1 letter and you can spell **slaw**. Some people like **slaw** on hot dogs.
8. Take 4 letters and spell **cars**. Most people drive **cars** or trucks.
9. Move the letters around and spell **scar**. I have a **scar** where I cut my chin.
10. Let's spell one 5-letter word, **crawl**. Worms and ants **crawl** along the road.
11. It's time for the secret word, and I bet you can figure it out. The baby **crawls** before it learns to walk.

Sort: Have the students pronounce all the words and sort them into rhyming patterns.

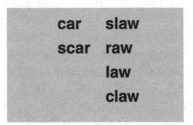

car	slaw
scar	raw
	law
	claw

Transfer: Show the students the two transfer words, **paw** and **draw**. Say to the students, "Let's pretend we are reading and come to these two new words." Have the students put the new words under the rhyming words and pronounce all the words.

Word Wall: Call out the five words added in lesson 70—**after, her, hurt, more,** and **some**. Have the students chant them, write them, and check them. Say the following words that rhyme with **more** and have the students spell them: **sore, tore, shore,** and **chore**.

Teach letter sounds: Remind the students about the sound of **aw** as in **saw**. Tell them that **al** can also make that sound.

Make Words:

1. Take 2 letters and spell the Word Wall word **in**.

2. Add a letter and spell **win**. <u>I hope our team will **win**.</u>

3. Let's start over and spell another 3-letter word, **law**. <u>She broke the **law** when she parked in the handicapped spot.</u>

4. Add a letter to spell **lawn**. <u>Who is going to mow the **lawn**?</u>

5. Start over and spell another 4-letter word, **king**. <u>In some countries, the **king** is the ruler.</u>

6. Change a letter to spell **wing**. <u>I sat over the **wing** of the airplane.</u>

7. Change just 1 letter and spell **wink**. <u>Can you **wink** at me?</u>

8. Change a letter and spell **link**. <u>The computer has a **link** to the Internet.</u>

9. Let's spell one more 4-letter word, **walk**. <u>I like to **walk**.</u>

10. Keep **walk**, add the remaining letters to it, and you will have the secret word. <u>**Walking** is wonderful exercise.</u>

Sort: First, have the students sort out **walk** and **walking** and make sentences with these two words. Make sure they notice that **walking** is **walk** with the ending **ing**. Next, have the students sort all the words into rhyming patterns.

| walk | | in | wing | wink |
| walking | | win | king | link |

Transfer: Show the students the two transfer words, **sting** and **stink**. Say to the students, "Let's pretend we are reading and come to these two new words." Have the students put the new words under the rhyming words and pronounce all the words.

Word Wall: Teach word endings by choosing **jump, jumping, hurt, stop,** and **ride**. Have the students chant them, write them, and check them. Then, have them add **ing** and write **hurting**, **stopping**, and **riding**. Remind them that sometimes spelling changes a little when we add endings to words. The **p** in **stop** is doubled when we add **ing**. When a word ends in **e** like **ride**, we drop the **e** and add **ing**.

Lesson 73

Letters: a e l l m s s t
Words: all mall tall tell sell salt stall smell small smallest

Make words: Have the students make these words and send one student to make the word with the big letters. Ask everyone to check their words and fix them if necessary.

1. Take 3 letters and spell **all**. I like it when you are **all** here.
2. Add a letter to spell **mall**. I like to shop at the **mall**.
3. Change 1 letter to spell **tall**. Most basketball players are very **tall**.
4. Change the vowel and you can spell **tell**. I will **tell** you a secret.
5. Change a letter and spell **sell**. I need to **sell** my old bike.
6. Let's spell one more 4-letter word, **salt**. Please pass the **salt**.
7. Take 5 letters and spell **stall**. Do you **stall** when it is bedtime?
8. Let's spell another 5-letter word, **smell**. I could **smell** the cake baking.
9. Change the vowel and spell **small**. I want just a **small** piece of cake.
10. Now it's time for the secret word. Add your remaining letters to the end of **small** and see what you have. That is the **smallest** piece of cake I have ever seen!

Sort: First, have the students sort out **small** and **smallest**. Help them notice that **smallest** is **small** with the ending **est**. Have the students use **small** and **smallest** in sentences. Next, have them sort all the words into rhyming patterns.

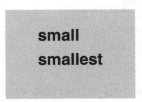

small
smallest

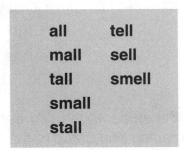

all	tell
mall	sell
tall	smell
small	
stall	

Transfer: Show the students the two transfer words, **wall** and **well**. Say to the students, "Let's pretend we are reading and come to these two new words." Have the students put the new words under the rhyming words and pronounce all the words.

Word Wall: Call out the Word Wall words **car, smart, for, sport,** and **more**. Have the students chant, write, and check them. Help them to notice the sound of **ar** in **car** and **smart** and the sound **or** in **for, sport,** and **more**.

Lesson 74

Letters: a e e u b c s
Words: us bus cue Sue sub cub cube base case cause because

Make words: Have the students make these words and send one student to make the word with the big letters. DO NOT wait for everyone to make the word before sending someone up. Ask everyone to check their words and fix them if necessary.

1. Let's start with a 2-letter word, **us**.
2. Add a letter to spell **bus**. She rides the **bus**.
3. Start over and spell another 3-letter word, **cue**. Listen for my **cue** and then come in.
4. Change the first letter and spell **Sue**. **Sue** is a name we have spelled lots of times.
5. Change the last letter and spell **sub**. When the teacher is out, you have a **sub**.
6. Change 1 letter to spell **cub**. A baby bear is called a **cub**.
7. Add a letter to **cub** to spell **cube**. I put an ice **cube** in my lemonade.
8. Start over and use 4 letters to spell **base**. The batter ran to first **base**.
9. Change the first letter and you can spell **case**. I carry my trumpet in its **case**.
10. Add a letter to **case** and spell **cause**. Watching scary movies may **cause** nightmares.
11. Now it's time for the secret word. Add your remaining letters to the front of **cause** and see what you have. I want to go **because** everyone else is going.

Sort: Have the students pronounce all the words and sort them into rhyming patterns.

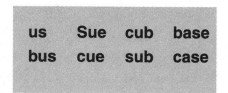

us	Sue	cub	base
bus	cue	sub	case

Transfer: Show the students the two transfer words, **chase** and **true**. Say to the students, "Let's pretend we are reading and come to these two new words." Have the students put the new words under the rhyming words and pronounce all the words.

Word Wall: Choose five starred words from the Word Wall for review. Have the students chant them, write them, and check them. If there is time, call out a few words that rhyme with and have the same pattern as the Word Wall words and have the students spell these new words.

Lesson 75

Word Wall Words: all because saw walk was
Secret Words: crawls walking smallest because
Letters and Sounds for Review: aw; au; al

To review the letters and sounds, the big letters for each secret word are put in the pocket chart and the students are invited to come and make words they remember from each lesson. (Students do not have their little individual letters.) Students should not try to make all the words from each lesson, but do have them make each secret word. Be sure they make the five words that will be added to the Word Wall.

Review:

1. Put the big letters **a, c, l, r, s,** and **w** in the pocket chart. Let students come and make any words they can. If no one makes **saw** and **was**, ask someone to come and make them. Show them the Word Wall cards for **saw** and **was**.

2. Remove the **c, r,** and **s** and add **i, g, k,** and **n**. If no one makes **walk**, ask someone to come and make it. Show them the Word Wall card for **walk**.

3. Remove the **i, g, k, n,** and **w** and add **e, l, m, s, s,** and **t**. Again, let students come and make some words. Be sure they make **all** and show them the Word Wall card for **all**.

4. Remove the **l, l, m, s,** and **t** and add **e, u, b,** and **c**. Again, let students come and make some words. Be sure they make **because** and show them the Word Wall card for **because**.

Word Wall:

1. Place the words on the Word Wall, have the students say each word, and use each word in a sentence. Be sure they notice that **all** and **saw** have stars.

2. Point to each new word and have the students chant its spelling three times in a rhythmic manner ("**o-n, on; o-n, on; o-n, on**").

3. Have the students write each new word as you model good writing using the board or overhead. Model and talk about correct letter formation as you write each word.

4. Have the students check their words by pointing to each letter and saying it aloud. Have them fix any words that need fixing.

5. If possible, give everyone a copy of the Take-Home Word Wall (page 172).

Lessons 76-80
Letters and Sounds: ou (as in cloud); ow (as in now and show)

Lesson 76

Letters: o u c d l s
Words: so do old sold cold loud cloud could scold clouds

Teach letter sounds: Have the students hold up their **o** and **u**. Tell them that some of the words they will make today will have the **ou** sound they hear in **out**. Have them make that sound.

Make words:

1. Let's start with a Word Wall word, **so**.
2. Change just the first letter and spell **do**. <u>**Do** you like school?</u>
3. Take 3 letters and spell **old**. <u>The **old** woman loved to tell stories.</u>
4. Add a letter and spell **sold**. <u>They **sold** all the tickets.</u>
5. Change 1 letter and spell **cold**. <u>In winter it gets very **cold**.</u>
6. Start over and use 4 letters to spell **loud**. <u>The fire alarm is very **loud**.</u>
7. Add a letter and spell **cloud**. <u>On a clear day there is not a **cloud** in the sky.</u>
8. Move around the letters in **cloud** and spell **could**. <u>We **could** go outside today.</u> **Could** has a strange spelling.
9. Spell one more 5-letter word, **scold**. <u>If you are late, your mother might **scold** you.</u>
10. It's secret word time. (You need to make one of the words we made and add your **s** to it.) <u>I looked at all the **clouds** and thought it would rain soon.</u>

Sort: Have the students pronounce all the words and sort them into rhyming patterns.

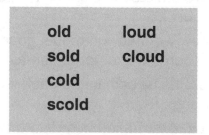

old	loud
sold	cloud
cold	
scold	

Transfer: Show the students the two transfer words, **proud** and **told**. Say to the students, "Let's pretend we are reading and come to these two new words." Have the students put the new words under the rhyming words and pronounce all the words.

Word Wall: Call out the five words added in lesson 75—**all, because, saw, walk,** and **was**. Have the students chant them, write them, and check them. Call out some rhyming words and have the students spell these: **fall, draw, claw, stall, and jaw**.

Lesson 77

Letters: a o b l l n s w
Words: was saw law low now snow slow ball allow snowball

Teach letter sounds: Have the students hold up their **o** and **w**. Tell them that **ow** can have the sound we hear in **now** and **slow**. Have them make both sounds.

Make words:

1. Take 3 letters and make **was**. I was walking home when I saw the dog.
2. Move the letters and spell **saw**. I saw (NAME) in the cafeteria.
3. Change 1 letter and spell **law**. I always try to obey the **law**.
4. Change the vowel and spell **low**. We went to the beach at **low** tide.
5. Change just 1 letter to spell **now**. Do it **now**! **Now** is spelled like **low**, but **ow** has a different sound. Let's say **low** and **now**.
6. Add a letter to **now** and spell **snow**. We love to play in the **snow**. Which **ow** sound do you hear in **snow**?
7. Change 1 letter and spell **slow**. The turtle is a very **slow** mover.
8. Start again and use 4 letters to spell **ball**. Throw the **ball** to me.
9. Now let's spell a 5-letter word, **allow**. My mom does not **allow** me to stay up late on school nights.
10. It's time for the secret word. I will give you a minute and then give you some clues. (It is a compound word that uses two of the words we have already made. It begins with **sn**.) She hit me with a **snowball**.

Sort: First, sort out **snow, ball,** and **snowball**, and help the students notice that **snowball** is a compound word. Have the students pronounce all the words and sort them into rhyming patterns.

snow		saw	slow	allow
ball		law	low	now
snowball			snow	

Transfer: Show the students the two transfer words, **show** and **plow**. Say to the students, "Let's pretend we are reading and come to these two new words." Tell the students that we don't know which **ow** pattern to use, so we will try it both ways and see which one makes a word we know.

Word Wall: Review word endings by choosing **jumping, stopped, things, ride,** and **skate**. Have the students chant them, write them, and check them. Then, have them add **ing, ed,** or **s** and write **rides, riding, skates, skated,** and **skating**. Remind them that when a word ends in **e** like **skate** or **ride**, we drop the **e** and add **ing**.

Lesson 78

Letters: o o l n p s w w
Words: now pow wow low owl owls slow snow plow snowplow

Teach letter sounds: Tell the students that today some of their words will need the **ow** they hear in **now** and some words will need the **ow** they hear in **slow**.

Make words:

1. Take 3 letters and spell **now**. <u>We need to go to lunch **now**.</u>
2. Change a letter to spell **pow**. <u>**Pow** is a word we see in comic books.</u>
3. Change a letter to spell **wow**. <u>**Wow**! That was a great movie!</u>
4. Change a letter and spell **low**. <u>Let's get down really **low** and hide behind this couch.</u>
5. Move the letters to spell **owl**. <u>An **owl** is a bird that comes out at night.</u>
6. Add a letter to spell **owls**. <u>A family of **owls** lives in that tree.</u>
7. Move the letters and you can spell **slow**. <u>**Slow** down!</u>
8. Change 1 letter to spell **snow**. <u>We had five inches of **snow**.</u>
9. Change the first 2 letters and spell **plow**. <u>In the spring, the farmer will **plow** his fields.</u>
10. It's time for the secret word. (It's a compound word that uses two of the words we made and begins with **sn**.) <u>The **snowplow** plowed our street and made big piles of snow on the sides.</u>

Sort: First, have the students sort out the words **snow, plow,** and **snowplow**. Have them notice that **snowplow** is a compound word, then have them make sentences with all three words. Finally, have the students pronounce all the words and sort them into rhyming patterns.

snow	
plow	
snowplow	

now	**low**
pow	**slow**
wow	**snow**
plow	

Transfer: Show the students the two transfer words, **grow** and **cow**. Say to the students, "Let's pretend we are reading and come to these two new words." Tell the students that we don't know which **ow** pattern to use, so we will try it both ways and see which one makes a word we know.

Word Wall: Call out **he, she, me, eat,** and **see**. Have the students chant, write, and check them. Help them to notice the sound of **e** in all the words and how that sound is spelled—**ea, ee,** or **e**.

Lesson 79

Letters: i o g g l n r w
Words: row low now owl girl gown glow grow growl growling

Make words:

1. Let's start with a 3-letter word, **row**. Put the chairs in a straight **row**.
2. Change the first letter to spell **low**. Let's crouch down really **low**.
3. Change the first letter to spell **now**. Can we eat **now**?
4. Use 3 letters to spell **owl**. I heard an **owl** hoot.
5. Start over and spell a 4-letter word, **girl**. The **girl** played soccer.
6. Let's spell another 4-letter word, **gown**. She wore a **gown** to the dance.
7. Take 4 letters and spell **glow**. She looked in the window and saw the **glow** of the fireplace.
8. Change 1 letter and spell **grow**. A kitten will **grow** very fast.
9. Add a letter to **grow** and spell **growl**. Did you hear that big dog **growl**?
10. Now it's time for the secret word. I bet someone will get it today. (Add your remaining letters to the word **growl**.) I heard the bears **growling** outside the tent.

Sort: Sort out **growl** and **growling** and have the students use both words in sentences. Have the students pronounce all the words and sort them into rhyming patterns.

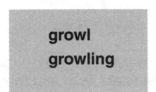

growl
growling

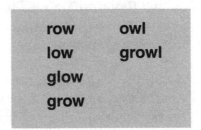

row	owl
low	growl
glow	
grow	

Transfer: Show the students the two transfer words, **howl** and **prowl**. Say to the students, "Let's pretend we are reading and come to these two new words." Have the students put the new words under the rhyming words and pronounce all the words.

Word Wall: Choose five starred words from the Word Wall for review. Have the students chant them, write them, and check them. Say five words that rhyme with and have the same pattern as the Word Wall words and have them spell these new words.

Lesson 80

Word Wall Words: cloud could girl now slow
Secret Words: clouds snowball snowplow growling
Letters and Sounds for Review: ou (as in cloud); ow (as in now and show)

To review the letters and sounds, the big letters for each secret word are put in the pocket chart and the students are invited to come and make words they remember from each lesson. (Students do not have their little individual letters.) Students should not try to make all the words from each lesson, but do have them make each secret word. Be sure they make the five words that will be added to the Word Wall.

Review:

1. Put the letters **o, u, c, d, l,** and **s** in the pocket chart. Let students come and make any words they can. Be sure they make **cloud** and **could** and show them the Word Wall cards for **cloud** and **could**.

2. Remove all the letters except **o** and **s**. Add **a, b, l, l, n,** and **w**. Again, let students come and make some words. Be sure they make **now** and **slow** and show them the Word Wall cards for **now** and **slow**.

3. Remove the **a, b,** and **l**. Add **o, p,** and **w**. Again, let students come and make some words.

4. Remove the **o, p, s,** and **w**. Add the **i, g, g,** and **r**. Again, let students come and make some words. Be sure they make **girl** and show them the Word Wall card for **girl**.

Word Wall:

1. Place the words on the Word Wall, have the students say each word, and use each word in a sentence. Be sure they notice that **now** and **slow** have stars, and that they are spelled the same but do not rhyme. Tell them that many words spelled **ow**, like **cow, how,** and **plow**, rhyme with **now**. Other **ow** words like **snow, show,** and **grow** rhyme with **slow**.

2. Point to each new word and have the students chant its spelling 3 times in a rhythmic manner.

3. Have the students write each new word as you model good writing using the board or overhead. Model and talk about correct letter formation as you write each word.

4. Have the students check their words by pointing to each letter and saying it aloud. Have them fix any words that need fixing.

5. If possible, give everyone a copy of the Take-Home Word Wall (page 173).

Lesson 81

Letters: i o o g m n z
Words: no go goo moo zoo zoom moon goon mooing zooming

Teach letter sounds: Have the students hold up their **z**, and tell them that today is the first time they will make words with the letter **z**. Tell them that **z** has the sound they hear at the beginning of **zoo** and have them make that sound. Next, have them hold up their two **o's**. Tell them that two **o's** together can have the sound they hear in **zoo** and that they will need to put the two **o's** together to make many of their words.

Make words:

1. Take 2 letters and make the Word Wall word, **no**.
2. Change 1 letter and make **go**. <u>We **go** to school every morning.</u>
3. Add a letter to go and you can spell **goo**. <u>In art class, I got **goo** all over my hands.</u>
4. Change 1 letter and you can spell **moo**. <u>I heard the cows **moo**.</u>
5. Change 1 letter and spell **zoo**. <u>We saw lots of animals at the **zoo**.</u>
6. Add 1 letter and you can spell **zoom**. <u>My new bike can **zoom** down the road.</u>
7. Let's spell another 4-letter word, **moon**. <u>There was a full **moon** last night.</u>
8. Change the first letter and spell **goon**. <u>I dreamed I was being chased by a **goon**.</u>
9. Add 2 letters and spell **mooing**. <u>Can you hear the cows **mooing**?</u>
10. It's time for the secret word, and I bet you can figure it out. (Start with the word **zoom** and see what you get when you add the remaining letters to it.) <u>We were **zooming** down the street on our bikes.</u>

Sort: Have the students pronounce all the words. First, have them sort out **moo, mooing, zoom,** and **zooming**. Help the students notice that **ing** was added to **moo** and **zoom** to spell the new words. Next, have them sort for rhyming patterns.

moo	zoom
mooing	zooming

no	moo	goon
go	goo	moon
	zoo	

Transfer: Show the students the two transfer words, **soon** and **spoon**. Say to the students, "Let's pretend we are reading and come to these two new words." Have the students put the new words under the rhyming words and pronounce all the words.

Word Wall: Call out the five words added in lesson 80—**cloud, could, girl, now,** and **slow**. Have the students chant them, write them, and check them. Remind them that **now** and **slow** have stars and that they are spelled the same, but do not rhyme. Have them spell **cow, how, snow, show,** and **grow**.

Lesson 82

Letters: e o o b f h k l s
Words: be elf boo book look hook fool shelf shook bookshelf

Teach letter sounds: Have the students hold up their two **o's**. Tell them that two **o's** together can have the sound they hear in **zoo** and the sound they hear in **look**. Have them say **look**. Today they will need to put the two **o's** together to spell the sound they hear in **look** and **zoo**.

Make Words:

1. Take 2 letters and spell the Word Wall word **be**.
2. Let's spell a 3-letter word, **elf**. When I was little, I played Santa's **elf** in a play.
3. Let's start over and spell another 3-letter word, **boo**. Boo is a word you say to scare someone.
4. Add a letter to spell **book**. That was a great **book**.
5. Change 1 letter and spell **look**. Look at my good writing.
6. Change a letter to spell **hook**. She put the bait on the **hook** and threw the **hook** into the water.
7. Now take 4 letters and spell **fool**. You can't **fool** me.
8. Now, let's spell a 5-letter word, **shelf**. Put the book on the **shelf**.
9. Let's spell one more 5-letter word, **shook**. The house **shook** when the wind blew hard.
10. Let's see if anyone has figured out the secret word. (It is a compound word that uses two words you made.) We have a **bookshelf** in the back of the room.

Sort: First, sort out **book, shelf,** and **bookshelf**. Have them notice that **bookshelf** is a compound word, then use all three words in a sentence. Next, have the students sort all the words into rhyming patterns.

book

shelf

bookshelf

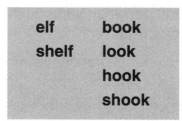

elf   book

shelf   look

       hook

       shook

Transfer: Show the students the two transfer words, **cook** and **took**. Say to the students, "Let's pretend we are reading and come to these two new words." Have the students put the new words under the rhyming words and pronounce all the words.

Word Wall: Teach the ending **er** by choosing the Word Wall words **players, walk, jump, ride,** and **skate**. Have the students chant them, write them, and check them. Tell them that **er** is an ending that shows a person or thing that does something: a **player plays**, a **skater skates**, etc. If you have more than one **player** or **skater**, you add the **s**. Have them add **er** or **ers** and write **jumper, riders, skaters, skater,** and **walkers**. Tell them that when a word ends in **e** like **skate** or **ride**, we just add the **r**.

Lesson 83

Letters: a o o b f l l t
Words: to too all fall ball tall tool fool foot football

Teach letter sounds: Have the students hold up their two **o's**. Remind them that two **o's** together can have the sound they hear in **zoo** and the sound they hear in **look**. Today they will make some words with the vowel sound they hear in **zoo** and some words with the vowel sound they hear in **look**.

Make words:

1. Take 2 letters and spell the Word Wall word, **to**. We drove from here **to** there.
2. Add a letter to spell another word, **too**. You use **too** when you complain that it is **too** hot, you are **too** tired, or you have **too** much work to do!
3. Now let's spell another Word Wall word, **all**. The cookies are **all** gone.
4. Add a letter and you can spell **fall**. Did you **fall** down?
5. Change a letter and spell **ball**. Let's play **ball**.
6. Change a letter again and spell **tall**. How **tall** are you?
7. Change 2 letters and spell **tool**. A hammer is a **tool**.
8. Change a letter and spell **fool**. She called me a **fool**.
9. Change a letter and spell **foot**. I hurt my **foot**.
10. Now it's time for the secret word. (Start with **foot** and add another word you made to spell a compound word.) We are going to the **football** game.

Sort: First, sort **foot, ball,** and **football**. Have the students notice that **football** is a compound word, then have them use all three words in a sentence. Have the students sort all the words into rhyming patterns.

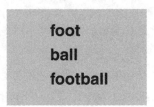

foot
ball
football

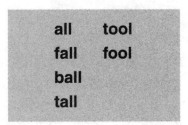

all   tool
fall   fool
ball
tall

Transfer: Show the students the two transfer words, **stall** and **pool**. Say to the students, "Let's pretend we are reading and come to these two new words." Have the students put the new words under the rhyming words and pronounce all the words.

Word Wall: Call out **girl, hurt, her, after,** and **player**. Have the students chant, write, and check them. Help them notice that **ir, ur,** and **er** can spell the same sound.

Lesson 84

Letters: e i c g h n w
Words: he we in win new hen when inch chin chew chewing

Teach letter sounds: Have the students hold up their **ew**. Tell them that **ew** sometimes has the sound they hear in **new**. Have them say **new**, and tell them today some of their words will have the vowel sound they hear in **new** and they will spell it with **ew**.

Make words:

1. Let's start with a Word Wall word, **he**.
2. Change a letter to spell **we**. We are making words.
3. Let's spell another Word Wall word, **in**.
4. Add a letter and spell **win**. Who do you think will **win**?
5. Start over and spell another 3-letter word, **new**. I have **new** sneakers.
6. Let's spell one more 3-letter word, **hen**. The **hen** lays eggs.
7. Add a letter to hen to spell **when**. When do we eat lunch?
8. Start over and use 4 letters to spell **inch**. He grew an **inch** in a month.
9. Move the letters around and you can spell **chin**. She bumped her **chin**.
10. Change the last 2 letters and spell **chew**. You need your teeth to **chew**.
11. Now it's time for the secret word. Add your remaining letters to the end of **chew** and see what you have. The old dog was **chewing** on a bone.

Sort: First, have the words **chew** and **chewing** sorted and have the students notice that **chewing** is **chew** with **ing**. Then, have the students sort all the words into rhyming patterns.

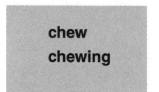

chew			
chewing			

he	in	chew	when
we	win	new	hen
	chin		

Transfer: Show the students the two transfer words, **spin** and **then**. Say to the students, "Let's pretend we are reading and come to these two new words." Have the students put the new words under the rhyming words and pronounce all the words.

Word Wall: Choose five starred words from the Word Wall for review. Have the students chant them, write them, and check them. Say a few words that rhyme with and have the same pattern as the Word Wall words and have the students spell these.

Lesson 85

Word Wall Words: too new look when zoo
Secret Words: zooming bookshelf football chewing
Letters and Sounds for Review: wh; z; oo (as in zoo and look); ew

To review the letters and sounds, the big letters for each secret word are put in the pocket chart and the students are invited to come and make words they remember from each lesson. (Students do not have their little individual letters.) Students should not try to make all the words from each lesson, but do have them make each secret word. Be sure they make the five words that will be added to the Word Wall.

Review:

1. Put the big letters **i, o, o, g, m, n,** and **z** in the pocket chart. Let students come and make any words they can. If no one makes **zoo**, ask someone to come and make it. Show them the Word Wall card for **zoo**.
2. Remove everything but the two **o's** and add **e, b, f, h, k, l,** and **s**. If no one makes **look**, ask someone to come and make it. Show them the Word Wall card for **look**.
3. Remove the **e, h, k,** and **s** and add **a, l,** and **t**. Again, let students come and make some words. Be sure they make **too** and show them the Word Wall card for **too**.
4. Remove all the letters and add **e, i, c, g, h, n,** and **w**. Again, let students come and make some words. Be sure they make **new** and **when** and show them the Word Wall cards for **new** and **when**.

Word Wall:

1. Place the words on the Word Wall, have the students say each word, and use each word in a sentence. Put a clue word next to **too** (big or little) to distinguish it from **to**. Tell the students that **too** is the word we use when something is **too** big, **too** little, or when we have **too** much. Have them use **to** and **too** in sentences. Review this often in the coming lessons as this is a difficult concept for most students. Be sure they notice the starred words **new**, **look**, and **when**.
2. Point to each new word and have the students chant its spelling three times in a rhythmic manner ("**o-n, on; o-n, on; o-n, on**").
3. Have the students write each new word as you model good writing using the board or overhead. Model and talk about correct letter formation as you write each word.
4. Have the students check their words by pointing to each letter and saying it aloud. Have them fix any words that need fixing.
5. If possible, give everyone a copy of the Take-Home Word Wall (page 174).

Lessons 86-90
Letters and Sounds: v; x; y; y (as in my and very)

Lesson 86

Letters: a e e d r s t y y
Words: yes yet set try dry are yard easy ready steady yesterday

Teach letter sounds: Have the students hold up their **y**. Tell them that **y** can have the sound they hear in **you**. Have them make that sound. Tell them that **y** can also be a vowel and can have the **i** sound in **my** and the **e** sound in **very**. Today, they will use the **y** to make all three sounds.

Make words:

1. Let's start with a 3-letter word, **yes**. <u>Yes, you may stay up late.</u>
2. Change just the last letter and spell **yet**. <u>Have you done your work **yet**?</u>
3. Change a letter and spell **set**. <u>Please **set** the table.</u>
4. Take 3 letters and spell **try**. <u>Do you like to **try** new foods?</u> Did you use your **y** to spell the **i** sound?
5. Change a letter and spell **dry**. <u>Put the dishes away when they are **dry**.</u>
6. Take 3 letters and spell **are**. <u>**Are** you almost ready?</u>
7. Start over and take 4 letters to spell **yard**. <u>The house had a big front **yard**.</u>
8. Now take 4 letters and spell **easy**. <u>**Easy** is not an **easy** word to spell.</u> Did you use your **y** to spell the **e** sound at the end of **easy**?
9. Now let's spell a 5-letter word, **ready**. <u>She is **ready** to go.</u>
10. Use 6 letters and spell **steady**. <u>Hold the board **steady** while I hammer in the nail.</u>
11. It's secret word time, and it's a hard one (Start with one **y** and end with the other **y**. This means the day before today.) <u>**Yesterday** we added words to the Word Wall.</u>

Sort: Have the students pronounce all the words and sort them into rhyming patterns.

yet	try	ready
set	dry	steady

Transfer: Show the students the two transfer words, **sly** and **met**. Say to the students, "Let's pretend we are reading and come to these two new words." Have the students put the new words under the rhyming words and pronounce all the words.

Word Wall: Call out the five words added in lesson 85—**too, new, look, when,** and **zoo**. Remind students that **too** is the word we use when we mean **too** big, **too** little, or **too** much. Have the students chant these words, write them, and check them. Then, have the students write five rhyming words: **hen, cook, shook, then,** and **brook**.

Lesson 87

Letters: e e i n s t x
Words: it sit six see seen teen next exit exist sixteen

Teach letter sounds: Have the students hold up their **x**. Tell them that only a few words (**X-ray, xylophone**) begin with **x,** but that words like **six** end with **x**. Have them say **six**.

Make words:

1. Take 2 letters and make **it**.
2. Add a letter and spell **sit**.
3. Change 1 letter and spell **six**. I invited **six** people to my party.
4. Now let's make a word you can all spell, **see**.
5. Add 1 letter to spell **seen**. Have you **seen** my red pencil?
6. Change a letter and spell **teen**. A **teen** is someone who is 13-19 years old.
7. Start over and spell **next**. Will you sit **next** to me on the bus?
8. Start again and use 4 letters to spell **exit**. We go out the **exit**.
9. Add 1 letter to **exit** and spell **exist**. Life cannot **exist** on any planet that does not have water. Let's stretch out **exist** and listen for what we need to add.
10. It's time for the secret word. I will give you a minute and then give you some clues. (Start with **six** and add another word you made.) My cousin just turned **sixteen**.

Sort: First, sort out **six, teen,** and **sixteen**, and help students notice that **sixteen** is a compound word. Have the students pronounce all the words and sort them into rhyming patterns.

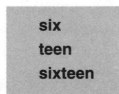

six

teen

sixteen

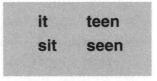

it   teen

sit   seen

Transfer: Show the students the two transfer words, **green** and **screen**. Say to the students, "Let's pretend we are reading and come to these two new words." Have the students put the new words under the rhyming words and pronounce all the words.

Word Wall: Call out the often confused words **was, saw, of, to,** and **too**. Remind students of the meanings of these words and use each word in a sentence. Have the students chant these words, write them, and check them. Then, say a sentence leaving a blank where the word should go. Have the students decide which word would make sense in the sentence and write the word again.

Lesson 88

Letters: a e e i l n n s t v
Words: an van vet vent vest nest sent vine vase valentines

Teach letter sounds: Have the students hold up their **v** and tell them that **v** makes the sound you hear at the beginning of **very**. Have everyone say **very**.

Make words: Have the students make these words and send one student to make the word with the big letters. Ask everyone to check their words and fix them if necessary.

1. Take 2 letters and spell **an**.
2. Add a letter to spell **van**. We all went in the **van**.
3. Let's spell another 3-letter word, **vet**. I took my dog to the **vet**.
4. Add a letter and spell **vent**. The heat comes out of the **vent**.
5. Change a letter to spell **vest**. The policeman wore a bulletproof **vest**.
6. Change a letter to spell **nest**. The **nest** was high up in the trees.
7. Move the letters and you can spell **sent**. I **sent** a package to my mom.
8. Start over and spell another 4-letter word, **vine**. Cucumbers grow on a **vine**.
9. Let's spell one more 4-letter word, **vase**. I put the flowers in a **vase**.
10. It's time for the secret word. (Start with your **v**. Think of a holiday that comes in February.)
    I sent **valentines** to all my friends.

Sort: First, have them sort the words that start with **v**. Next, have the students sort all the words into rhyming patterns.

van		
vent		
vet		
vine		
vest		
vase		
valentines		

an	sent	nest
van	vent	vest

Transfer: Show the students the two transfer words, **chest** and **spent**. Say to the students, "Let's pretend we are reading and come to these two new words." Have the students put the new words under the rhyming words and pronounce all the words.

Word Wall: Call out the often confused words **when, there, this, to,** and **too**. Remind the students of the meanings of the words and use each word in a sentence. Have the students chant them, write them, and check them. Then, say a sentence leaving a blank where the word should go. Have the students decide which word would make sense in the sentence and write the word again.

Lesson 89

Letters: e e o b d r v y y
Words: by dry boy Roy body over ever very every everybody

Make words:

1. Let's start with a 2-letter word, **by**. <u>The cat stood **by** his dish waiting for food.</u>
2. Let's spell a 3-letter word, **dry**. <u>Are the clothes **dry** yet?</u>
3. Now spell another 3-letter word, **boy**. <u>(NAME) is a **boy**.</u>
4. Change the first letter and spell a name, **Roy**. <u>**Roy** is my friend.</u>
5. Add a letter to spell **body**. <u>I try to take care of my **body**.</u>
6. Start over and spell another 4-letter word, **over**. <u>Pour the sauce **over** the spaghetti.</u>
7. Change 1 letter and spell **ever**. <u>Did you **ever** see a rabbit that big?</u>
8. Take 4 letters and spell **very**. <u>The cookies were **very** good.</u>
9. Add 1 letter and spell **every**. <u>**Every** cookie got gobbled up.</u>
10. Now it's time for the secret word. I bet someone will get it today. (Put two of the words you made together to make a compound word.) <u>**Everybody** is trying to figure out the secret word.</u>

Sort: Sort out **every, body,** and **everybody** and have the students notice that **everybody** is a compound word made with **every** and **body**. Have the students use all three words in sentences. Have the students sort all the words into rhyming patterns.

every
body
everybody

by	boy
dry	Roy

Transfer: Show the students the two transfer words, **toy** and **shy**. Say to the students, "Let's pretend we are reading and come to these two new words." Have the students put the new words under the rhyming words and pronounce all the words.

Word Wall: Choose five starred words from the Word Wall for review. Have the students chant them, write them, and check them. Say five words that rhyme with and have the same pattern as the five Word Wall words and have the students spell these new words.

Lesson 90

Word Wall Words: are dry six over very
Secret Words: yesterday sixteen valentines everybody
Letters and Sounds for Review: v; x; y; y (as in my and very)

To review the letters and sounds, the big letters for each secret word are put in the pocket chart and the students are invited to come and make words they remember from each lesson. (Students do not have their little individual letters.) Students should not try to make all the words from each lesson, but do have them make each secret word. Be sure they make the five words that will be added to the Word Wall.

Review:

1. Put the letters **a, e, e, d, r, s, t, y,** and **y** in the pocket chart. Let students come and make any words they can. Be sure they make **are** and **dry** and show them the Word Wall cards for **are** and **dry**.
2. Remove all the letters except **e, e, s,** and **t.** Add **i, n,** and **x.** Again, let students come and make some words. Be sure they make **six** and show them the Word Wall card for **six**.
3. Remove the **x.** Add **a, l, n,** and **v.** Again, let students come and make some words.
4. Remove all the letters except the **e, e,** and **v.** Add the **o, b, d, r, y,** and **y.** Again, let students come and make some words. Be sure they make **over** and **very** and show them the Word Wall cards for **over** and **very**.

Word Wall:

1. Place the words on the Word Wall, have the students say each word, and use each word in a sentence. **Dry** is the only starred word.
2. Point to each new word and have the students chant its spelling three times in a rhythmic manner.
3. Have the students write each new word as you model good writing using the board or overhead. Model and talk about correct letter formation as you write each word.
4. Have the students check their words by pointing to each letter and saying it aloud. Have them fix any words that need fixing.
5. If possible, give everyone a copy of the Take-Home Word Wall (page 175).

Lessons 91-95
Letters and Sounds: qu; c (as in centers); g (as in gym)

Lesson 91

Letters: e i o u n q s t
Words: to in it sit into note quit quiet quite quote question

Teach letter sounds: Have the students hold up their **q** and **u**. Tell the students that **qu** has the sound they hear at the beginning of **question**. Have them say **question**. Tell them that some of the words they make today will need the **qu**.

Make words: Have the students make these words and send one student to make the word with the big letters. Ask everyone to check their words and fix them if necessary.

1. Let's start with a Word Wall word, **to**.
2. Let's spell another Word Wall word, **in**.
3. Let's spell another Word Wall word, **it**.
4. Add a letter and spell **sit**.
5. Let's spell a 4-letter word, **into**. We went **into** the house.
6. Start over and take 4 letters to spell **note**. I wrote a thank-you **note** to my grandma for my birthday gift.
7. Let's spell another 4-letter word, **quit**. My friend got mad and **quit** the team.
8. Add a letter to **quit** and spell **quiet**. It is very **quiet** in here. Let's all stretch out **quiet** and listen for the letters we hear.
9. Move the letters around and spell **quite**. I am not **quite** ready yet.
10. Change the vowel and spell **quote**. When you **quote** someone, you say exactly what they said.
11. It's secret word time. This is a hard one and the ending has a strange spelling. (Begin your word with **qu**. Put **tion** at the end. **Tion** says "shun." This is something you ask.) Does anybody have a **question**?

Sort: Have the students sort **in**, **to**, and **into** and notice that **into** is a compound word made up of **in** and **to**. Next, have them sort all the words into rhyming patterns.

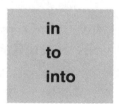

in		it	quote
to		sit	note
into		quit	

Transfer: Show the students the two transfer words, **vote** and **fit**. Say to the students, "Let's pretend we are reading and come to these two new words." Have the students put the new words under the rhyming words and pronounce all the words.

Word Wall: Call out the five words added in lesson 90—**are, dry, six, over,** and **very**. Have the students chant them, write them, and check them. Then, have them write five words that rhyme with **dry**: **by, my, try, fry,** and **fly**.

Lesson 92

Letters: e e c n r s t
Words: see tree nest sent cent rent enter center secret centers

Teach letter sounds: Have the students hold up their **c**. Tell them that in many words **c** has the sound you hear in **car**. Tell them that **c** can also have an **s** sound as it does in the word **centers**. Have them say **centers** and tell them that the **s** sound they hear at the beginning is spelled with a **c**. Tell students that some of the words they spell today will use the **c** to spell the **s** sound.

Make words:

1. Take 3 letters and make **see**.
2. Now let's spell a 4-letter word, **tree**. We sat under the **tree**.
3. Start over and spell another 4-letter word, **nest**. The birds were building a **nest**.
4. Move the letters around and spell **sent**. He **sent** me some money.
5. Change just 1 letter to spell another **cent**, the **cent** that is the same as a penny. I spent all the money and don't have a single **cent** left! This **cent** spells the **s** sound with the letter **c**.
6. Change a letter and spell **rent**. The **rent** on this apartment is very high.
7. Now let's spell a 5-letter word, **enter**. You can't go out that door because it says, "**Enter**." Let's all stretch out **enter** and listen for the letters.
8. Add a letter to **enter** to spell **center**. My aunt goes to the senior citizen's **center**.
9. Let's spell one more 6-letter word, **secret**. I won't tell the **secret**. Let's all stretch out **secret**.
10. It's time for the secret word. I will give you a minute and then give you some clues. (Add **s** to one of the words we made and you will have it.) We like to do things in the **centers**.

Sort: Have the students pronounce all the words and sort them into rhyming patterns.

see	rent	enter
tree	sent	center
	cent	

Transfer: Show the students the two transfer words, **went** and **free**. Say to the students, "Let's pretend we are reading and come to these two new words." Have the students put the new words under the rhyming words and pronounce all the words.

Word Wall: Review word endings by choosing **cloud, look, girl, float,** and **use**. Have the students chant them, write them, and check them. Then, have the students write **users, floating, girls, looked,** and **clouds**.

Lesson 93

Letters: a i u g m m n s y
Words: my an any may say Sam gym man many gymnasium

Teach letter sounds: Have the students hold up their **g**. Tell them that in many words **g** has the sound you hear in **girl**. Tell them that **g** can also have a **j** sound as it does in the word **gym**. Have students say **gym** and tell them that the **j** sound they hear at the beginning is spelled with a **g**. Tell them that some of the words they spell today will use the **g** to spell the **j** sound..

Make words:

1. Take 2 letters and spell **my**. My **name** is (NAME).
2. Use 2 letters to spell **an**. **An** apple tastes good.
3. Add a letter to spell **any**. I don't want **any** soup.
4. Let's spell another 3-letter word, **may**. You **may** go back to your seats now.
5. Change a letter to spell **say**. What did she **say**?
6. Change a letter to spell **Sam**. I gave the books to **Sam**. Did you remember to use a capital **S**?
7. Now we need to use the **g** to make the **j** sound and the **y** for the vowel to spell **gym**. We play games in the **gym**. **Gym** has a funny spelling, but it is a fun place.
8. Let's spell another 3-letter word, **man**. The **man** will bring the pizza at 2:00.
9. Add a letter and spell **many**. **Many** people love pizza.
10. It's time for the secret word. It's a hard one today, so I will give you some clues. (Start with **gym** and then add letters to spell the whole name of the **gym**.) The whole name of the gym is **gymnasium**.

Sort: First, sort out **gym** and **gymnasium** and tell the students that many long words can be shortened to short words. The **TV** is really a **television**. The **Net** is really the **Internet**. Next, have the students sort all the words into rhyming patterns.

gym		
gymnasium		

an	any	may
man	many	say

Transfer: Show the students the two transfer words, **spray** and **plan**. Say to the students, "Let's pretend we are reading and come to these two new words." Have the students put the new words under the rhyming words and pronounce all the words.

Word Wall: Call out **those, float, slow, no,** and **over**. Have the students chant, write, and check these words. Help the students notice the sound of **o** in all the words and how that sound is spelled— **ow, oa, o-e,** or **o**.

Lesson 94

Letters: e e o b f r
Words: be of or for bee fee free robe bore before

Make words: Have the students make these words and send one student to make the word with the big letters. Ask everyone to check their words and fix them if necessary.

1. Let's start with the Word Wall word, **be**.
2. Let's spell another Word Wall word, **of**.
3. Let's spell another Word Wall word, **or**.
4. Add a letter to spell yet another Word Wall word, **for**.
5. Start over and spell a 3-letter word, **bee**. This **bee** is the kind that can sting you.
6. Change the first letter and spell **fee**. We had to pay a **fee** to play.
7. Add a letter and spell **free**. I wish we could go and play for **free**.
8. Start again and spell another 4-letter word, **robe**. When it's cold, I put on a **robe** over my pajamas.
9. Move the letters around and spell **bore**. I hope the long speech will not **bore** you.
10. Now it's time for the secret word. I bet someone will get it today. (Start with the word **be**. This is the opposite of after.) Please get home **before** it gets dark.

Sort: Have the students pronounce all the words and sort them into rhyming patterns.

Transfer: Show the students the two transfer words, **store** and **shore**. Say to the students, "Let's pretend we are reading and come to these two new words." Have the students put the new words under the rhyming words and pronounce all the words.

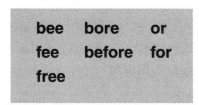

bee	bore	or
fee	before	for
free		

Word Wall: Choose five starred words from the Word Wall for review. Have the students chant them, write them, and check them. Say five words that rhyme with and have the same pattern as the Word Wall words and have the students spell these new words.

Lesson 95

Word Wall Words: before centers gym my question
Secret Words: question centers gymnasium before
Letters and Sounds for Review: qu; c (as in centers); g (as in gym)

To review the letters and sounds, the big letters for each secret word are put in the pocket chart and the students are invited to come and make words they remember from each lesson. (Students do not have their little individual letters.) Students should not try to make all the words from each lesson, but do have them make each secret word. Be sure they make the five words that will be added to the Word Wall.

Review:

1. Put the letters **e, i, o, u, n, q, s,** and **t** in the pocket chart. Let students come and make any words they can. Be sure they make **question** and show them the Word Wall card for **question**.
2. Remove all the letters except **e, n, t,** and **s**. Add **e, c,** and **r**. Again, let students come and make some words. Be sure they make **centers** and show them the Word Wall card for **centers**.
3. Remove all the letters except **n** and **s**. Add **a, i, u, g, m, m,** and **y**. Again, let students come and make some words. Be sure they make **my** and **gym** and show them the Word Wall cards for **my** and **gym**.
4. Remove all the letters. Add the **e, e, o, b, f,** and **r**. Again, let students come and make some words. Be sure they make **before** and show them the Word Wall card for **before**.

Word Wall:

1. Place the words on the Word Wall, have the students say each word, and use each word in a sentence. **My** is the only starred word.
2. Point to each new word and have the students chant its spelling three times in a rhythmic manner.
3. Have the students write each new word as you model good writing using the board or overhead. Model and talk about correct letter formation as you write each word.
4. Have the students check their words by pointing to each letter and saying it aloud. Have them fix any words that need fixing.
5. If possible, give everyone a copy of the Take-Home Word Wall (page 176).

Lessons 96–100
Letters and Sounds: bl; br; pl; pr; sl

Lesson 96

Letters: a o b b l p r y
Words: by boy Roy pro pry pay pray play baby probably

Teach letter sounds: Have the students hold up their **p** and their **r**. Tell them that many of the words they make today will begin with the letters **pr**.

Make words:

1. Take 2 letters and spell **by**. I walked **by** (NAME'S) house.
2. Add 1 letter and spell **boy**.
3. Change 1 letter and spell **Roy**. Roy is a basketball player.
4. Start over and spell another 3-letter word, **pro**. He is a real **pro**.
5. Change 1 letter and spell **pry**. I need a screw driver to **pry** open this box.
6. Let's spell one more 3-letter word, **pay**. I will **pay** you to mow my lawn.
7. Add a letter and spell **pray**. I **pray** that it won't rain on the day of our picnic.
8. Change 1 letter and spell **play**. We will **play** games at the picnic.
9. Spell one more 4-letter word, **baby**. The **baby** cried all night.
10. It's secret word time. (Start with **pr** and put **y** at the end. This is a word that means maybe.) I will **probably** get to come to the picnic.

Sort: First, have the students sort out all the words that begin with **pr** and say them, emphasizing the **pr** sound at the beginning. Next, have the students sort all the words into rhyming patterns.

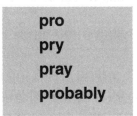

pro
pry
pray
probably

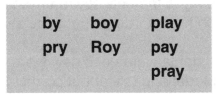

by	boy	play
pry	Roy	pay
		pray

Transfer: Show the students the two transfer words, **stay** and **toy**. Say to the students, "Let's pretend we are reading and come to these two new words." Have the students put the new words under the rhyming words and pronounce all the words.

Word Wall: Call out the five words added in lesson 95—**before, centers, gym, my,** and **question**. Have the students chant them, write them, and check them. Remind the students that **c** usually has the **k** sound we hear at the beginning of **car**, but can also have the **s** sound we hear at the beginning of **centers**. **G** usually has the sound we hear at the beginning of **girl**, but can sound like **j** as it does in **gym**. **Qu** has the sound we hear at the beginning of **question**. Say some words that begin like **centers, gym,** or **question** and let students decide the letters with which these new words begin: **circus, quit, giraffe, general, cycle,** and **quack**.

Letters: a o u d g l n p r y
Words: pray play plan plug glad grad grand groan group proud glory playground

Teach letter sounds: Have the students hold up their **p** and their **r**. Tell them that many of the words they make today will begin with the letters **pr**. Repeat this as they hold up **pl, gr,** and **gl**.

Make words: Have the students make these words and send one student to make the word with the big letters. Ask everyone to check their words and fix them if necessary.

1. Take 4 letters and make **pray**.
2. Change 1 letter and spell **play**.
3. Change the last letter and spell **plan**. <u>Let's **plan** what we will do at the picnic.</u>
4. Change the last 2 letters and spell **plug**. <u>We need a **plug** to keep the water in the tub.</u>
5. Start over and use 4 letters to spell **glad**. <u>I was **glad** when they fixed the air conditioner.</u>
6. Change 1 letter and spell **grad**. <u>We call someone who has just graduated a **grad**.</u>
7. Add 1 letter and spell **grand**. <u>We had a **grand** time at the picnic.</u>
8. Start again and use 5 letters to spell **groan**. <u>Some people **groan** when they get out of bed in the morning.</u>
9. Change the last 2 letters and spell **group**. <u>Can I join your **group**?</u>
10. Let's spell another 5-letter word, **proud**. <u>You should be **proud** of how quickly you can spell words.</u>
11. Now let's spell one more 5-letter word, **glory**. <u>The winners get all the **glory**.</u>
12. It's time for the secret word. I will give you a minute and then give you some clues. (Begin your word with **play** and think of someplace you like to play.) <u>Let's go to the **playground**.</u>

Sort: First, have the students sort out all the words that begin with **pr, pl, gr,** and **gl** and say them, emphasizing the sounds at the beginnings of the words. Next, have the students sort all the words into rhyming patterns.

pray	play		grad	glad
proud	plan		grand	glory
	plug		group	
	playground		groan	

pray	glad
play	grad

Transfer: Show the students the two transfer words, **sad** and **way**. Say to the students, "Let's pretend we are reading and come to these two new words." Have the students put the new words under the rhyming words and pronounce all the words.

Word Wall: Call out these often confused words: **could, are, very, to,** and **too**. Remind the students of the words' meanings and use each word in a sentence. Have the students chant them, write them, and check them. Then, say a sentence leaving a blank where the word should go. Have the students decide which word would make sense in each sentence and write the word again.

Lesson 98

Letters: e i u b b d l r s
Words: blue blur bled sled slid slide bride bribe bridle bruise bluebirds

Teach letter sounds: Have the students hold up their **s** and their **l**. Tell them that many of the words they make today will begin with the letters **sl**. Repeat this as they hold up **bl** and **br**.

Make words:

1. Take 4 letters and spell **blue**. <u>**Blue** is one of my favorite colors.</u>
2. Change 1 letter to spell **blur**. <u>When I take my glasses off, everything is a **blur**.</u>
3. Change the last 2 letters to spell **bled**. <u>His cut foot **bled** all over the rug.</u>
4. Change 2 letters to spell **sled**. <u>I went down the hill on my **sled**.</u>
5. Change the vowel to spell **slid**. <u>We **slid** into a big pile of snow.</u>
6. Add a letter and you can spell **slide**. <u>We love to **slide** in the snow.</u>
7. Change 2 letters to spell **bride**. <u>The **bride** walked down the aisle.</u>
8. Change 1 letter and spell **bribe**. <u>The man was arrested for taking a **bribe**.</u>
9. Now, let's spell a 6-letter word, **bridle**. <u>We need to put the saddle and the **bridle** on the horse before we can ride.</u>
10. Let's spell another 6-letter word, **bruise**. <u>I got a big **bruise** on my arm from falling out of the tree.</u>
11. It's time for the secret word. (It's a compound word that begins with **blue** and is a type of bird.) <u>The **bluebirds** sang and flew around the yard.</u>

Sort: First, have the students sort out all the words that begin with **bl, br,** and **sl** and say them, emphasizing the beginning sounds. Next, have the students sort all the words into rhyming patterns.

blue	bride	sled
blur	bribe	slid
bled	bridle	slide
bluebirds	bruise	

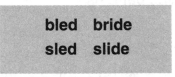

Transfer: Show the students the two transfer words, **pride** and **Fred**. Say to the students, "Let's pretend we are reading and come to these two new words." Have the students put the new words under the rhyming words and pronounce all the words.

Word Wall: Call out **I, ride, night, my,** and **dry**. Have the students chant, write, and check these words. Help the students notice the sound of **i** in all the words and how that sound is spelled—**igh, i, i-e,** or **y**.

Teach letter sounds: Have the students hold up their **s** and their **l**. Tell them that many of the words they make today will begin with the letters **sl**. Repeat this as they hold up **bl** and **br**.

Make words:

1. Let's start with a 3-letter word, **sad**. <u>Why are you **sad**?</u>
2. Add a letter to spell **said**. <u>She **said** she would come right over.</u>
3. Let's spell another 4-letter word, **Brad**. <u>**Brad** likes to bowl.</u>
4. Let's spell one more 4-letter word, **slid**. <u>We **slid** on the ice.</u>
5. Now spell a 5-letter word, **slick**. <u>When the rain froze, all the roads were very **slick**.</u>
6. Change 2 letters and spell **brick**. <u>He lives in a **brick** house.</u>
7. Change 1 letter and spell **brisk**. <u>It was a chilly, **brisk** morning.</u>
8. Start over and use 5 letters to spell **slack**. <u>The fishing line was **slack** until the fish took the bait.</u>
9. Change 2 letters and spell **black**. <u>The dog was white with **black** spots.</u>
10. Now it's time for the secret word. (This is another kind of bird that starts with **black**.) <u>The **blackbirds** were flying south.</u>

Sort: First, have the students sort out all the words that begin with **br, bl,** and **sl**. Next, have them say these words, emphasizing the beginning sounds. Finally, have the students sort all the lesson words into rhyming patterns.

Brad	black	slid
brick	blackbirds	slack
brisk		slick

sad	brick	slack
Brad	slick	black

Transfer: Show the students the two transfer words, **track** and **trick**. Say to the students, "Let's pretend we are reading and come to these two new words." Have the students put the new words under the rhyming words and pronounce all the words.

Word Wall: Choose five starred words from the Word Wall for review. Have the students chant them, write them, and check them. Say five words that rhyme with and have the same pattern as the Word Wall words and have the students spell these new words.

Lesson 100

Word Wall Words: black boy glad probably said
Secret Words: probably playground bluebirds blackbirds
Letters and Sounds for Review: bl; br; pl; pr; sl

To review the letters and sounds, the big letters for each secret word are put in the pocket chart and the students are invited to come and make words they remember from each lesson. (Students do not have their little individual letters.) Students should not try to make all the words from each lesson, but do have them make each secret word. Be sure they make the five words that will be added to the Word Wall.

Review:

1. Put the letters **a, o, b, b, l, p, r,** and **y** in the pocket chart. Let students come and make any words they can. Be sure they make **boy** and **probably** and show them the Word Wall cards for **boy** and **probably**.
2. Remove the **b** and **b**. Add **u, d, g,** and **n**. Again, let students come and make some words. Be sure they make **glad** and show them the Word Wall card for **glad**.
3. Remove the **a, o, g, n, p,** and **y**. Add **e, i, b, b,** and **s**. Again, let students come and make some words.
4. Remove the **e** and **u**. Add the **a, c,** and **k**. Again, let students come and make some words. Be sure they make **said** and **black** and show them the Word Wall cards for **said** and **black**.

Word Wall:

1. Place the words on the Word Wall, have the students say each word, and use each word in a sentence. **Black, boy,** and **glad** are starred words.
2. Point to each new word and have the students chant its spelling three times in a rhythmic manner.
3. Have the students write each new word as you model good writing using the board or overhead. Model and talk about correct letter formation as you write each word.
4. Have the students check their words by pointing to each letter and saying it aloud. Have them fix any words that need fixing.
5. If possible, give everyone a copy of the Take-Home Word Wall (page 177).

Lessons 101-105
Letters and Sounds: cl; cr; gl; gr; tr

Lesson 101

Letters: a i c g l n p p
Words: lap lip pan pain clip clap clan plan plain cling clapping

Teach letter sounds: Have the students hold up their **c** and their **l**. Tell them that many of the words they make today will begin with the letters **cl**. Repeat this as they hold up **pl**.

Make words:

1. Let's start with a 3-letter word, **lap**. <u>The cat slept in my **lap**.</u>
2. Change the vowel and spell **lip**. <u>It hurt when I bit my **lip**.</u>
3. Let's spell another 3-letter word, **pan**. <u>The **pan** is very hot.</u>
4. Add 1 letter and spell **pain**. <u>He was in a lot of **pain** after the accident.</u>
5. Let's spell another 4-letter word, **clip**. <u>I need a paper **clip**.</u>
6. Change the vowel and spell **clap**. <u>We will all **clap** when the play is over.</u>
7. Change the last letter and spell **clan**. <u>The two friends were members of the same **clan**.</u>
8. Change 1 letter and spell **plan**. <u>We need to **plan** what we are going to do.</u>
9. Add 1 letter and spell **plain**. <u>I like **plain** vanilla ice cream, with nothing added.</u>
10. Start over and spell another 5-letter word, **cling**. <u>A scared child will **cling** to his mother.</u>
11. It's secret word time. (Begin your word with **clap** and add the other letters.) <u>Everybody was</u> **clapping** <u>when I finished the song.</u>

Sort: First, have the students sort out all the words that begin with **pl** and **cl**. Next, have the students say the **pl** and **cl** words, emphasizing the sounds at the beginnings of the words. Finally, have the students sort all the lesson words into rhyming patterns.

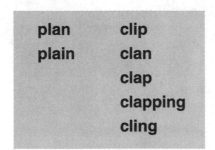

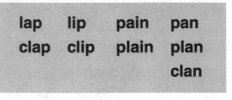

Transfer: Show the students the two transfer words, **brain** and **ship**. Say to the students, "Let's pretend we are reading and come to these two new words." Have the students put the new words under the rhyming words and pronounce all the words.

Word Wall: Call out the five words added in lesson 100—**black, glad, boy, probably,** and **said**. Have the students chant them, write them, and check them. Have them spell the rhyming words: **snack, toy, mad, sad,** and **shack**.

Lesson 102

Letters: a i c d d g h l n r
Words: clan grin grad glad gland grand grind grain cling child grandchild

Teach letter sounds: Have the students hold up their **c** and their **l**. Tell them that many of the words they make today will begin with the letters **cl**. Repeat this as they hold up **gl** and **gr**.

Make words:

1. Take 4 letters and make **clan**. We are in the same **clan**.
2. Now let's spell another 4-letter word, **grin**. The happy boy had a big **grin** on his face.
3. Change the last 2 letters and spell another 4-letter word, **grad**. The new **grad** was looking for a job.
4. Change 1 letter and spell **glad**. He was **glad** when he found a good job.
5. Add 1 letter to spell **gland**. His throat hurt because his **gland** was swollen.
6. Change 1 letter and spell **grand**. We had a **grand** time on our trip.
7. Change 1 letter and spell **grind**. It makes a loud noise when they **grind** the coffee beans into coffee.
8. Change the last 3 letters to spell **grain**. Cereals are made of **grain**.
9. Let's spell another 5-letter word, **cling**. Most baby animals **cling** to their mothers.
10. Let's spell one more 5-letter word, **child**. The **child** did not want her mother to leave.
11. It's time for the secret word. I will give you a minute and then give you some clues. (Put two of your words together to make a compound word.) We have one **grandchild**.

Sort: First, have the students sort out all the words that begin with **cl, gl,** and **gr**. Next, have the students say the **cl, gl,** and **cr** words, emphasizing the sounds at the beginnings of the words. Finally, have the students sort all the lesson words into rhyming patterns.

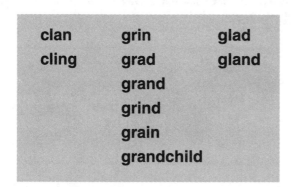

clan	grin	glad
cling	grad	gland
	grand	
	grind	
	grain	
	grandchild	

grad	grand
glad	gland

Transfer: Show the students the two transfer words, **stand** and **mad**. Say to the students, "Let's pretend we are reading and come to these two new words." Have the students put the new words under the rhyming words and pronounce all the words.

Word Wall: Call out **black, brother, player, probably,** and **slow**. Have the students chant, write, and check these words. Tell them that these words are on the Word Wall to help them remember the sounds for **bl, br, pl, pr,** and **sl**. Say the following words that begin with these letters and ask the students which two letters they would use to begin writing these words: **bread, plastic, slippery, blast, program, blue, sleepy, plan, breakfast,** and **promise**.

Teach letter sounds: Have the students hold up their **c** and their **r**. Tell them that many of the words they make today will begin with the letters **cr**. Repeat this as they hold up **tr**.

Make words:

1. Take 4 letters and spell **tree**. The boys built a house in the big **tree**.
2. Change 1 letter to spell **true**. I am going to tell you a **true** story.
3. Start over and use 4 letters to spell **race**. (NAME) won the **race**.
4. Let's spell another 4-letter word, **rust**. There was **rust** all over the old truck.
5. Add 1 letter to spell **crust**. The cheesecake has a graham cracker **crust**.
6. Use 5 letters to spell **trace**. We **trace** around shapes to make pictures.
7. Move the letters in **trace** to spell **crate**. The bike came in a big **crate**.
8. Add 1 letter to **crate** to spell **crater**. The **crater** was a huge hole caused by a volcano.
9. Move the letters and spell **create**. We like to **create** buildings with the blocks.
10. Use eight of your letters to spell **treasure**. We were looking for buried **treasure**.
11. It's time for the secret word. It's a hard one today so I will give you some clues. (Start with **cr** and end with **tures**. Sometimes you see these in scary movies.) I had nightmares about the **creatures** in the scary movie.

Sort: First, have the students sort out all the words that begin with **cr** and **tr**. Next, have the students say the **cr** and **tr** words, emphasizing the sounds at the beginnings of the words. Finally, have the students sort all the lesson words into rhyming patterns.

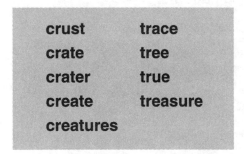

crust	trace
crate	tree
crater	true
create	treasure
creatures	

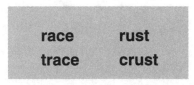

race	rust
trace	crust

Transfer: Show the students the two transfer words, **trust** and **face**. Say to the students, "Let's pretend we are reading and come to these two new words." Have the students put the new words under the rhyming words and pronounce all the words.

Word Wall: Call out **look, slow, now, oil,** and **boy**. Have the students chant, write, and check these words. Help the students notice the sound of **oo** in **look**, **ow** in **slow** and **now**, **oi** in **oil**, and **oy** in **boy**. Have them spell the rhyming words **throw, brow, brook, broil,** and **joy**.

Lesson 104

Letters: e e i g h n r t v y
Words: ten try tree grin teen then they there their green greet everything

Teach letter sounds: Have the students hold up their **t** and their **r**. Tell them that many of the words they make today will begin with the letters **tr**. Repeat this as they hold up **gr**.

Make words:

1. Let's start with a 3-letter word, **ten**. We have **ten** fingers.
2. Let's spell another 3-letter word, **try**. We all **try** to figure out the secret word.
3. Let's spell a 4-letter word, **tree**. The **tree** is huge.
4. Start over and spell another 4-letter word, **grin**. Can you **grin** like a monkey?
5. Use 4 letters to spell **teen**. A teenager is sometimes called a **teen**.
6. Start over and use 4 letters and spell **then**. We watched a movie, **then** we went to bed.
7. Change 1 letter and spell **they**. **They** all went to the game.
8. Let's spell a Word Wall word, **there**. The girls are over **there**.
9. Now use 5 letters to spell a different **their**. This **their** is a word we use to show that something belongs to someone. The students took **their** lunches on the bus.
10. Start over and spell another 5-letter word, **green**. **Green** is my favorite color.
11. Change 1 letter and spell **greet**. She went to the door to **greet** the visitors.
12. Now it's time for the secret word. It's a hard one and I will give you some clues. (It's a compound word that starts with **e** and ends with **ing**. It means all the things.) When I am hungry, I want to eat **everything**.

Sort: First, have the students sort the words that begin with **tr** and **gr**. Then, have the students pronounce all the lesson words and sort them into rhyming patterns.

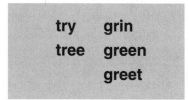

try	grin
tree	green
	greet

ten	teen
then	green

Transfer: Show the students the two transfer words, **screen** and **pen**. Say to the students, "Let's pretend we are reading and come to these two new words." Have the students put the new words under the rhyming words and pronounce all the words.

Word Wall: Choose five starred words from the Word Wall for review. Have the students chant them, write them, and check them. Say five words that rhyme with and have the same pattern as the Word Wall words and have the students spell these new words.

Lesson 105

Word Wall Words: creatures green their then they
Secret Words: clapping grandchild creatures everything
Letters and Sounds for Review: cl; cr; gl; gr; tr

To review the letters and sounds, the big letters for each secret word are put in the pocket chart and the students are invited to come and make words they remember from each lesson. (Students do not have their little individual letters.) Students should not try to make all the words from each lesson, but do have them make each secret word. Be sure they make the five words that will be added to the Word Wall.

Review:

1. Put the letters **a, i, c, g, l, n, p,** and **p** in the pocket chart. Let students come and make any words they can.
2. Remove **p** and **p**. Add **d, d, h,** and **r**. Again, let students come and make some words.
3. Remove all the letters except **a, c,** and **r**. Add **e, e, u, r, s,** and **t**. Again, let students come and make some words. Be sure they make **creatures** and show them the Word Wall card for **creatures**.
4. Remove all the letters except **e, e, r,** and **t**. Add the **i, g, h, n, v,** and **y**. Again, let students come and make some words. Be sure they make **green, their, then,** and **they** and show them the Word Wall cards for **green, their, then,** and **they**.

Word Wall:

1. Place the words on the Word Wall, have the students say each word, and use each word in a sentence. Put a clue word next to **their** (car) to distinguish it from **there**. Tell the students that **their** is the word we use when something belongs to someone. <u>Their car belongs to them.</u> Have students use **there** and **their** in sentences. Review this often in the coming lessons as this is a difficult concept for most of the students. Help them notice they have one starred word, **then**.
2. Point to each new word and have the students chant its spelling three times in a rhythmic manner.
3. Have the students write each new word as you model good writing using the board or overhead. Model and talk about correct letter formation as you write each word.
4. Have the students check their words by pointing to each letter and saying it aloud. Have them fix any words that need fixing.
5. If possible, give everyone a copy of the Take-Home Word Wall (page 178).

Lessons 106-110
Letters and Sounds: dr; fl; sn; sp

Lesson 106

Letters: a i o d n r s s t w
Words: do dot not two said rain want draw down drown drain downstairs

Teach letter sounds: Have the students hold up their **d** and their **r**. Tell them that many of the words they make today will begin with the letters **dr**.

Make words:

1. Take 2 letters and spell **do**. <u>**Do** you like making words?</u>
2. Add 1 letter and spell **dot**. <u>A period is a little **dot** we put at the end of sentences.</u>
3. Change 1 letter and spell **not**. <u>(NAME) was **not** here yesterday.</u>
4. Start over and spell another 3-letter word, **two**. This **two** is not the **too** big **too** and not the go **to** school **to**. This is the number **two** and it begins like twins and twice. <u>The **two** babies are twins.</u>
5. Now, let's spell a 4-letter word, **said**. **Said** has a funny spelling in the middle. <u>The teacher **said** we are very smart.</u>
6. Let's spell another 4-letter word, **rain**. <u>**Rain** is good for plants and trees.</u>
7. Start over and spell **want**. <u>I **want** a new bike for my birthday.</u>
8. Let's spell another 4-letter word, **draw**. <u>**Draw** a picture to illustrate your story.</u>
9. Spell one more 4-letter word, **down**. <u>We walked **down** the road.</u>
10. Add 1 letter to **down** and spell **drown**. <u>I can swim so I know I won't **drown** in the deep end of the pool.</u>
11. Spell one more 5-letter word, **drain**. <u>Take the plug out and let the water **drain** out of the bathtub.</u>
12. It's secret word time. (It's a compound word. The first part of the compound word is **down**.) <u>The library is **downstairs**.</u>

Sort: First, have the students sort out all the words that begin with **dr**. Next, have the students say the **dr** words, emphasizing the **dr** sound at the beginnings of the words. Finally, have the students sort all the lesson words into rhyming patterns.

drain	
drown	
draw	

dot	drain	drown
not	rain	down

Transfer: Show the students the two transfer words, **brain** and **spot**. Say to the students, "Let's pretend we are reading and come to these two new words." Have the students put the new words under the rhyming words and pronounce all the words.

Word Wall: Call out the five words added in lesson 105—**creatures, green, their, then,** and **they**. Remind the students that **their** is the **their** we use to show something belongs to someone. Have the students chant, write, and check the five newest Word Wall words.

Lesson 107

Letters: a i o d p n r r s
Words: sap spa spin snip snap drip drop drain Spain sprain raindrops

Teach letter sounds: Have the students hold up their **d** and their **r**. Tell them that some of the words they make today will begin with the letters **dr**. Repeat this as they hold up **sp** and **sn**.

Make words:

1. Take 3 letters and make **sap**. Sap is sticky and comes from trees.
2. Move the letters and spell **spa**. She went to a health **spa** for vacation.
3. Now let's spell a 4-letter word, **spin**. If you **spin** around too much, you can get dizzy.
4. Move the letters and spell **snip**. Use your scissors and **snip** off the top of the shape.
5. Change 1 letter to spell **snap**. Can you **snap** your fingers?
6. Start over and spell another 4-letter word **drip**. Turn the faucet off so it doesn't **drip**.
7. Change 1 letter and spell **drop**. Be careful you don't **drop** that glass.
8. Now use 5 letters to spell **drain**. I like to watch the water **drain** out of the tub.
9. Change just the first 2 letters and spell the country of **Spain**. Someday I would love to go to **Spain**.
10. Add 1 letter and spell **sprain**. Sometimes when you fall, you **sprain** your ankle.
11. It's time for the secret word. I will give you a minute and then give you some clues. (It's a compound word and starts with **rain**.) I like listening to the **raindrops** landing on the roof.

Sort: First, have the students sort out all the words that begin with **dr, sn,** and **sp**. Next, have the students say the **dr, sn,** and **sp** words, emphasizing the sounds at the beginnings of the words. Finally, have the students sort all the lesson words into rhyming patterns.

drip	snip	spin
drop	snap	spa
drain		Spain
		sprain

sap	snip	Spain
snap	drip	drain
		sprain

Transfer: Show the students the two transfer words, **ship** and **chain**. Say to the students, "Let's pretend we are reading and come to these two new words." Have the students put the new words under the rhyming words and pronounce all the words.

Word Wall: Call out some often confused words—**too, two, they, there,** and **their**. Remind the students of the meanings of the words, and use each word in a sentence. Have the students chant them, write them, and check them. Then, say a sentence, leaving a blank where one of these words should go. Have the students decide which word would make sense in the sentence and write the word again.

Lesson 108

Letters: a e o f k l n s s w
Words: saw slaw slow flow flew snow flake snake sneak fleas floss snowflakes

Teach letter sounds: Have the students hold up their **s** and their **l**. Tell them that many of the words they make today will begin with the letters **sl**. Repeat this as they hold up **sn** and **fl**.

Make words:

1. Take 3 letters and spell **saw**. I **saw** a good movie last weekend.
2. Add 1 letter to spell **slaw**. Do you like **slaw** on your hot dogs?
3. Change 1 letter to spell **slow**. Turtles are **slow** animals.
4. Change 1 letter to spell **flow**. The water in the stream will **flow** down the hill.
5. Change the vowel to spell **flew**. We **flew** to California on a jet plane.
6. Let's spell one more 4-letter word, **snow**. Do you like to play in the **snow**?
7. Let's spell a 5-letter word, **flake**. I saw the first **flake** of snow.
8. Change 2 letters and spell **snake**. A **snake** is a reptile.
9. Move the letters around and spell **sneak**. Do you ever try to **sneak** into the house when you are late?
10. Let's spell another 5-letter word, **fleas**. My dog needs a bath because she has **fleas**.
11. Let's spell another 6-letter word, **floss**. You need to brush and **floss** your teeth.
12. It's time for the secret word. (It's a compound word that begins with **snow** and uses another word we made.) The **snowflakes** fell so fast the whole world was white.

Sort: First, have the students sort out all the words that begin with **fl, sn,** and **sl**. Next, have the students say the **fl, sn,** and **sl** words, emphasizing the sounds at the beginnings of the words. Finally, have the students sort all the lesson words into rhyming patterns.

flow	snow	slaw
flew	snake	slow
flake	sneak	
fleas	snowflakes	
floss		

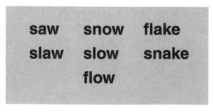

saw	snow	flake
slaw	slow	snake
	flow	

Transfer: Show the students the two transfer words, **grow** and **claw**. Say to the students, "Let's pretend we are reading and come to these two new words." Have the students put the new words under the rhyming words and pronounce all the words.

Word Wall: Call out **cloud, creatures, glad, green,** and **train**. Have the students chant, write, and check these words. Tell them that these words are on the Word Wall to help them remember the sounds for **cl, cr, gl, gr,** and **tr**. Say the following words beginning with these letters, and ask the students which two letters they would use to begin writing these words: **trick, grass, clippers, crash, glue, glass, treasure, grade, class,** and **cross**.

Lesson 109
Letters: e u b f l r t t y
Words: but flu fly fry try true blue flute turtle butter butterfly

Teach letter sounds: Have the students hold up their **t** and their **r**. Tell them that many of the words they make today will begin with the letters **tr**. Repeat this as they hold up **fl**.

Make words: Have the students make these words and send one student to make the word with the big letters. Ask everyone to check their words and fix them if necessary.

1. Let's start with a 3-letter word, **but**. I want to buy a book, **but** I spent all my money.
2. Start over and spell another 3-letter word, **flu**. Every year I get a **flu** shot because I don't want to get the **flu**.
3. Change 1 letter and spell **fly**. Do you wish you could **fly**?
4. Change 1 letter and spell **fry**. Do you know how to **fry** eggs?
5. Change 1 letter and spell **try**. Do you like to **try** new foods?
6. Let's spell a 4-letter word, **true**. I am going to tell you a **true** story.
7. Change 2 letters and spell **blue**. Is **blue** your favorite color?
8. Start over and use 5 letters to spell **flute**. My sister plays the **flute**.
9. Now, let's start over and spell a 6-letter word, **turtle**. I had a pet **turtle**.
10. Let's spell another 6-letter word, **butter**. I put **butter** on my toast.
11. Now it's time for the secret word. (It's a compound word that uses two of the words we made today.) A caterpillar turns into a **butterfly**.

Sort: First, have the students sort out all the words that begin with **fl** and **tr**. Next, have the students say the **fl** and **tr** words, emphasizing the sounds at the beginnings of the words. Finally, have the students sort all the lesson words into rhyming patterns.

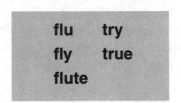

flu	try
fly	true
flute	

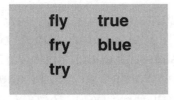

fly	true
fry	blue
try	

Transfer: Show the students the two transfer words, **shy** and **due**. Say to the students, "Let's pretend we are reading and come to these two new words." Have the students put the new words under the rhyming words and pronounce all the words.

Word Wall: Choose five starred words from the Word Wall for review. Have the students chant them, write them, and check them. Say five words that rhyme with and have the same pattern as the Word Wall words and have the students spell these new words.

Lesson 110

Word Wall Words: but do not snake want
Secret Words: downstairs raindrops snowflakes butterfly
Letters and Sounds for Review: dr; fl; sn; sp

To review the letters and sounds, the big letters for each secret word are put in the pocket chart and the students are invited to come and make words they remember from each lesson. (Students do not have their little individual letters.) Students should not try to make all the words from each lesson, but do have them make each secret word. Be sure they make the five words that will be added to the Word Wall.

Review:

1. Put the letters **a, i, o, d, n, r, s, s, t,** and **w** in the pocket chart. Let students come and make any words they can. Be sure they make **do, not,** and **want** and show them the Word Wall cards for **do, not,** and **want**.
2. Remove the **s, t,** and **w**. Add **p** and **r**. Again, let students come and make some words.
3. Remove the **i, d, r,** and **r**. Add **e, f, k, l, s,** and **w**. Again, let students come and make some words. Be sure they make **snake** and show them the Word Wall card for **snake**.
4. Remove all the letters except **e, f,** and **l**. Add **u, b, r, t, t,** and **y**. Again, let students come and make some words. Be sure they make **but** and show them the Word Wall card for **but**.

Word Wall:

1. Place the words on the Word Wall, have the students say each word, and use each word in a sentence. **But**, **not**, and **snake** are starred words.
2. Point to each new word and have the students chant its spelling three times in a rhythmic manner.
3. Have the students write each new word as you model good writing using the board or overhead. Model and talk about correct letter formation as you write each word.
4. Have the students check their words by pointing to each letter and saying it aloud. Have them fix any words that need fixing.
5. If possible, give everyone a copy of the Take-Home Word Wall (page 179).

Lesson 111

Letters: a a e c c h r r s t
Words: cat scat scar star stare scare crash crate crater characters

Teach letter sounds: Have the students hold up their **c** and their **r**. Tell them that many of the words they make today will begin with the letters **cr**. Repeat this as they hold up **sc** and **st**.

Make words:

1. Let's start with a 3-letter word, **cat**. The **cat** slept in my lap.
2. Add 1 letter and spell **scat**. I told the cat to **scat.**
3. Change 1 letter and spell **scar**. I have a **scar** on my chin from when I fell off my bike.
4. Change 1 letter and spell **star**. She was the **star** of the show.
5. Add 1 letter and spell **stare**. Please don't **stare** at me.
6. Change 1 letter and spell **scare**. Do not let those silly monsters **scare** you.
7. Start over and spell another 5-letter word, **crash**. I saw the car **crash** into the fence.
8. Change 3 letters and spell **crate**. I wonder what is in that big **crate**?
9. Add 1 letter to **crate** and spell **crater**. A **crater** is a large hole.
10. It's secret word time. (Begin with **ch** and end with **s**. Stories have these, and they are very important.) The **characters** are the people in the story.

Sort: First, have the students sort out all the words that begin with **cr, sc,** and **st**. Next, have the students say the **cr, sc,** and **st** words, emphasizing the sounds at the beginnings of the words. Finally, have the students sort all the lesson words into rhyming patterns.

crash	scat	star
crate	scar	stare
crater	scare	

cat	star	stare
scat	scar	scare

Transfer: Show the students the two transfer words, **dare** and **brat**. Say to the students, "Let's pretend we are reading and come to these two new words." Have the students put the new words under the rhyming words and pronounce all the words.

Word Wall: Call out the five words added in lesson 110—**but, do, not, snake,** and **want**. Have the students chant them, write them, and check them. Then, have the students spell the rhyming words **shut, shot, shake, flake,** and **quake**.

Lesson 112

Letters: a e e r s t w
Words: saw tar star were stew steer stare straw sweet sweat sweater

Teach letter sounds: Have the students hold up their **s** and their **w**. Tell them that many of the words they make today will begin with the letters **sw**. Repeat this as they hold up **st**.

Make words:

1. Let's start with the Word Wall word **saw**. I saw that movie three times.
2. Now let's spell another 3-letter word, **tar**. The tar on the road was hot and sticky.
3. Add 1 letter and spell star. That star is very bright.
4. Use 4 letters to spell **were**. Were you at school yesterday?
5. Start over and use 4 letters to spell **stew**. I like beef stew.
6. Use 5 letters to spell **steer**. It is hard to steer a car on a mountain road.
7. Now, let's spell **stare**. I tried not to stare at the funny-looking man.
8. Let's spell one more 5-letter word, **straw**. The first little pig built a straw house.
9. Use 5 letters to spell **sweet**. The candy was very sweet.
10. Let's spell one more 5-letter word, **sweat**. I sweat when I run in the summer.
11. It's time for the secret word. I will give you a minute and then give you some clues. (Start with **sweat** and add your other letters.) Where is my sweater?

Sort: First, have the students sort out all the words that begin with **sw** and **st**. Next, have the students say the **sw** and **st** words, emphasizing the sounds at the beginnings of the words. Finally, have the students sort all the lesson words into rhyming patterns.

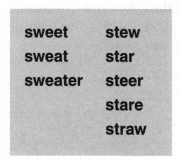

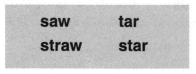

Transfer: Show the students the two transfer words, **far** and **claw**. Say to the students, "Let's pretend we are reading and come to these two new words." Have the students put the new words under the rhyming words and pronounce all the words.

Word Wall: Call out **dry, float, friend, snake,** and **sport**. Have the students chant, write, and check them. Tell the students that these words are on the Word Wall to help them remember the sounds for **dr, fl, fr, sn,** and **sp**. Say the following words beginning with those letters and ask the students which two letters they would use to begin writing these words: **snore, special, fresh, flat, driveway, drop, floor, sparkles, snap,** and **France**.

Lesson 113

Letters: e i d f l n r y
Words: fly fry dry red Fred fled fine line fried friend friendly

Teach letter sounds: Have the students hold up their **f** and their **r**. Tell them that many of the words they make today will begin with the letters **fr**. Repeat this as they hold up **fl**.

Make words: Have the students make these words and send one student to make the word with the big letters. Ask everyone to check their words and fix them if necessary.

1. Take 3 letters and spell **fly**. <u>I wish I could **fly**.</u>
2. Change 1 letter to spell **fry**. <u>Let's **fry** some chicken.</u>
3. Start over and use 3 letters to spell **dry**. <u>Are the clothes **dry** yet?</u>
4. Let's spell another 3-letter word, **red**. <u>I love **red** roses.</u>
5. Add 1 letter to spell **Fred**. <u>**Fred** is my neighbor.</u>
6. Change 1 letter to spell **fled**. <u>The robbers **fled** from the bank.</u>
7. Start over and spell another 4-letter word **fine**. <u>It was a **fine** day.</u>
8. Change 1 letter to spell **line**. <u>Let's **line** up for lunch.</u>
9. Use 5 letters to spell **fried**. <u>I love **fried** chicken.</u>
10. Add 1 letter to spell **friend**. <u>My best **friend** is coming to visit me.</u>
11. It's time for the secret word. (Start with **friend** and add your other letters.) <u>Your dog is very **friendly**.</u>

Sort: First, have the students sort out **fry/fried** and **friend/friendly** and talk about how the words are related. Next, have the students sort all the words that begin with **fr** and **fl**. Then, have the students say the **fr** and **fl** words, emphasizing the sounds at the beginnings of the words. Finally, have the students sort all the words into rhyming patterns.

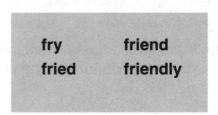

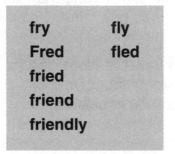

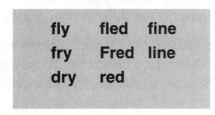

Transfer: Show the students the two transfer words, **shine** and **shed**. Say to the students, "Let's pretend we are reading and come to these two new words." Have the students put the new words under the rhyming words and pronounce all the words.

Word Wall: Review word endings by choosing **want, boy, question, snake,** and **skate**. Have students chant these words, write them, and check them. Then, have the students write **skaters, boys, wanting, questioned,** and **snakes.**

Lesson 114

Letters: e o u f l r s y
Words: of fry fly sly yes elf you your four yourself

Make words:

1. Let's start with a Word Wall word, **of**. <u>Please cut me a piece **of** cake.</u>
2. Let's spell a 3-letter word, **fry**. <u>Do you know how to **fry** eggs?</u>
3. Change 1 letter and spell **fly**. <u>I know an old lady who swallowed a **fly**.</u>
4. Change 1 letter and spell **sly**. <u>We read a story about a **sly**, old fox.</u>
5. Use 3 letters to spell **yes**. <u>**Yes**, you can go to the party.</u>
6. Now, let's spell **elf**. <u>An **elf** is an imaginary helper.</u>
7. Let's spell one more 3-letter word, **you**. <u>**You** are all good at spelling words.</u>
8. Add 1 letter to **you** and spell **your**. <u>This is **your** seat.</u>
9. Change 1 letter and spell **four**. This **four** is the number **four**. <u>I wish I had **four** brothers and **four** sisters.</u>
10. Now, it's time for the secret word. (It's a compound word that starts with the word **your**.) <u>Today, I want you to read by **yourself**.</u>

Sort: Have the students pronounce all the words and sort them into rhyming patterns.

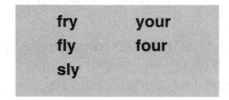

fry	your
fly	four
sly	

Transfer: Show the students the two transfer words, **pour** and **sky**. Say to the students, "Let's pretend we are reading and come to these two new words." Have the students put the new words under the rhyming words and pronounce all the words.

Word Wall: Choose five starred words from the Word Wall for review. Have the students chant them, write them, and check them. Say five words that rhyme with and have the same pattern as the Word Wall words, and have the students spell these new words.

Word Wall Words: scare sweater were you your
Secret Words: characters sweater friendly yourself
Letters and Sounds for Review: fr; sc; st; sw

To review the letters and sounds, the big letters for each secret word are put in the pocket chart and the students are invited to come and make words they remember from each lesson. (Students do not have their little individual letters.) Students should not try to make all the words from each lesson, but do have them make each secret word. Be sure they make the five words that will be added to the Word Wall.

Review:

1. Put the letters **a, a, e, c, c, h, r, r, s,** and **t** in the pocket chart. Let students come and make any words they can. Be sure they make **scare** and show them the Word Wall card for **scare**.
2. Remove all the letters except **a, e, r, s,** and **t**. Add **e** and **w**. Again, let students come and make some words. Be sure they make **were** and **sweater** and show them the Word Wall cards for **were** and **sweater**.
3. Remove all the letters except **e** and **r**. Add **i, d, f, l, n,** and **y**. Again, let students come and make some words.
4. Remove all the letters except **e, f, l, r,** and **y**. Add the **o, u, and s**. Again, let students come and make some words. Be sure they make **you** and **your** and show them the Word Wall cards for **you** and **your**.

Word Wall:

1. Place the words on the Word Wall, have the students say each word, and use each word in a sentence. There are no starred words.
2. Point to each new word and have the students chant its spelling three times in a rhythmic manner.
3. Have the students write each new word as you model good writing using the board or overhead. Model and talk about correct letter formation as you write each word.
4. Have the students check their words by pointing to each letter and saying it aloud. Have them fix any words that need fixing.
5. If possible, give everyone a copy of the Take-Home Word Wall (page 180).

Lessons 116-120
Letters and Sounds: sk; sm

Lesson 116

Letters: a e l l m r s
Words: am arm are Sam all mall sell smell small smear smaller

Teach letter sounds: Have the students hold up their **s** and their **m**. Tell them that many of the words they make today will begin with the letters **sm**.

Make words:

1. Take 2 letters and spell **am**. I am hungry.
2. Add 1 letter and spell **arm**. I wear a watch on my **arm**.
3. Now, let's spell the Word Wall word, **are**. **Are** you glad to be here today?
4. Start over and spell another 3-letter word, **Sam**. **Sam** is my cousin.
5. Let's spell another Word Wall word, **all**. I know you can **all** spell **all**.
6. Add another letter and spell **mall**. I like to shop at the **mall**.
7. Let's spell one more 4-letter word, **sell**. Let's **sell** the car and buy a truck.
8. Add 1 letter to **sell** and spell **smell**. I could **smell** the pizza, and it made me hungry.
9. Change 1 letter and spell **small**. My house is very **small**.
10. Let's spell one more 5-letter word, **smear**. Let the paint dry so it won't **smear**.
11. It's secret word time. (Start with **small**. Add your other letters.) My house is **smaller** than your house.

Sort: First, have the students sort out **small** and **smaller** and talk about how the words are related. Next, have the students sort all the words that begin with **sm**. Then, have the students say the **sm** words, emphasizing the **sm** sound at the beginnings of the words. Finally, have the students sort all the words into rhyming patterns.

small
smaller

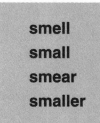

smell
small
smear
smaller

am	all	smell
Sam	mall	sell
	small	

Transfer: Show the students the two transfer words, **stall** and **shell**. Say to the students, "Let's pretend we are reading and come to these two new words." Have the students put the new words under the rhyming words and pronounce all the words.

Word Wall: Call out the five words added in lesson 115—**scare, sweater, were, you,** and **your**. Have the students chant them, write them, and check them. Then, say a sentence leaving a blank where one of these words should go. Have the students decide which word would make sense in the sentence and write the word again.

Lesson 117

Letters: i k n n s y
Words: is in inn ink kin sky ski skin sink skinny

Teach letter sounds: Have the students hold up their **s** and their **k**. Tell them that many of the words they make today will begin with the letters **sk**.

Make words:

1. Let's start with the Word Wall word, **is**.
2. Let's spell another Word Wall word, **in**.
3. Add 1 letter and spell the **inn** that is a motel. We stayed at the Holiday Inn®.
4. Change 1 letter and spell **ink**. You can write this letter with your **ink** pen.
5. Move the letters around and spell **kin**. Sometimes we talk about our relatives as our **kin**.
6. Start over and spell another 3-letter word, **sky**. The **sky** is blue and clear today.
7. Change 1 letter and spell **ski**. In the winter, I like to **ski**.
8. Add 1 letter and spell **skin**. She had a fever, and her **skin** was very hot.
9. Move the letters around to spell **sink**. Some things **sink** and other things float.
10. It's time for the secret word. I will give you a minute and then give you some clues. (Start with **skin** and add your other letters.) The **skinny** cat was looking for food.

Sort: First, have the students sort out **skin** and **skinny** and talk about how they are related. Next, have the students sort out the words that begin with **sk**. Finally, have the students sort all the words into rhyming patterns.

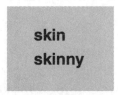

skin skinny	sky ski skin skinny	in ink kin sink skin

Transfer: Show the students the two transfer words, **think** and **stink**. Say to the students, "Let's pretend we are reading and come to these two new words." Have the students put the new words under the rhyming words and pronounce all the words.

Word Wall: Call out these often confused words: **was, saw, want, when,** and **very**. Remind the students of the meanings of the words, and use each word in a sentence. Have the students chant them, write them, and check them. Then, say a sentence leaving a blank where one of the words should go. Have the students decide which word would make sense in the sentence and write the word again.

Lesson 118

Letters: a e b r r r s t w y
Words: say stay sway brew stew star stray straw sweat sweaty strawberry

Teach letter sounds: Have the students hold up their **s** and their **t**. Tell them that many of the words they make today will begin with the letters **st**. Repeat this as they hold up **sw**.

Make words:

1. Take 3 letters and spell **say**. What did you **say**?
2. Add 1 letter to spell **stay**. I want to **stay** a little longer.
3. Change 1 letter to spell **sway**. Trees **sway** in the wind.
4. Let's spell another 4-letter word, **brew**. The witches were stirring the **brew**.
5. Change 2 letters to spell **stew**. Do you like chicken **stew**?
6. Let's spell one more 4-letter word, **star**. The **star** was shining brightly in the sky.
7. Let's spell a 5-letter word, **stray**. We adopted a **stray** dog.
8. Change 1 letter and you can spell **straw**. The basket was made of **straw**.
9. Start over and spell another 5-letter word, **sweat**. The air conditioner went off and we all began to **sweat**.
10. Add 1 letter and spell **sweaty**. We got all **sweaty**.
11. It's time for the secret word. It's a hard one. I will give you some clues. (Start with a word you made, **straw**. Add letters to spell something good to eat.) I love **strawberry** pie.

Sort: First, have the students sort out **sweat** and **sweaty** and use these words in a sentence. Next, have the students sort out all the words that begin with **st** and **sw**. Then, have the students say the **st** and **sw** words, emphasizing the sounds at the beginnings of the words. Finally, have the students sort all the lesson words into rhyming patterns.

sweat	stay	sway		say	stew
sweaty	stew	sweat		stay	brew
	star	sweaty		sway	
	stray			stray	
	straw				
	strawberry				

Transfer: Show the students the two transfer words, **chew** and **spray**. Say to the students, "Let's pretend we are reading and come to these two new words." Have the students put the new words under the rhyming words and pronounce all the words.

Word Wall: Choose five starred words from the Word Wall for review. Have the students chant them, write them, and check them. Say five words that rhyme with and have the same pattern as the Word Wall words, and have the students spell these new words.

Lesson 119

Letters: e i o g h m n s t
Words: go get his him Tim them home nose those night might something

Make words:

1. Let's start with a Word Wall word, **go**.
2. Now spell a 3-letter word, **get**. Every year I **get** a flu shot.
3. Take 3 letters and spell **his**. (NAME) always does **his** work.
4. Change 1 letter and spell **him**. Give the money to **him**.
5. Change 1 letter and spell **Tim**. **Tim** is Tom's brother.
6. Let's spell a 4-letter word, **them**. Can you take their books to **them**?
7. Use 4 letters to spell **home**. I am going **home**.
8. Start over and use 4 letters to spell **nose**. The puppy's **nose** was cold.
9. Now, spell a 5-letter word, **those**. Please hand me **those** papers.
10. Now, let's spell a 5-letter Word Wall word, **night**. The fire started during the **night**.
11. Change 1 letter and spell **might**. We **might** play outside today.
12. Now, it's time for the secret word. (It's a compound word that uses two of the Word Wall words. The first part is **some**.) I am looking for **something** good.

Sort: Have the students sort all the words into rhyming patterns.

him	those	night
Tim	nose	might

Transfer: Show the students the two transfer words, **light** and **fright**. Say to the students, "Let's pretend we are reading and come to these two new words." Have the students put the new words under the rhyming words and pronounce all the words.

Word Wall: Choose five starred words from the Word Wall for review. Have the students chant them, write them, and check them. Say five words that rhyme with and have the same pattern as the Word Wall words and have the students spell these new words.

Lesson 120

Word Wall Words: go get him smaller them
Secret Words: smaller skinny strawberry something
Letters and Sounds for Review: sk; sm

To review the letters and sounds, the big letters for each secret word are put in the pocket chart and the students are invited to come and make words they remember from each lesson. (Students do not have their little individual letters.) Students should not try to make all the words from each lesson, but do have them make each secret word. Be sure they make the five words that will be added to the Word Wall.

Review:

1. Put the letters **a, e, l, l, m, r,** and **s** in the pocket chart. Let students come and make any words they can. Be sure they make **smaller** and show them the Word Wall card for **smaller**.
2. Remove all the letters except **s**. Add **i, k, n, n,** and **y**. Again, let students come and make some words.
3. Remove all the letters except **s** and **y**. Add **a, e, b, r, r, r, t,** and **w**. Again, let students come and make some words.
4. Remove all the letters except **e, s,** and **t**. Add the **e, i, o, g, h, m,** and **n**. Again, let students come and make some words. Be sure they make **go, get, him,** and **them** and show them the Word Wall cards for **go, get, him,** and **them**.

Word Wall:

1. Place the words on the wall, have the students say each word, and use each word in a sentence. **Get** and **him** are starred words.
2. Point to each new word and have the students chant its spelling three times in a rhythmic manner.
3. Have the students write each new word as you model good writing using the board or overhead. Model and talk about correct letter formation as you write each word.
4. Have the students check their words by pointing to each letter and saying it aloud. Have them fix any words that need fixing.
5. If possible, give everyone a copy of the Take-Home Word Wall (page 181).

Lessons 121-125
Letters and Sounds: Review

Lesson 121

Letters: e o h r s s w
Words: we he she how who rose sore shore horses showers

Make words:

1. Let's start with a 2-letter word **we**. <u>**We** are making words.</u>
2. Let's spell a Word Wall word, **he**.
3. Let's spell another Word Wall word, **she**.
4. Take 3 letters and spell **how**. <u>**How** are you?</u>
5. Move the letters around and spell **who**. <u>**Who** wants to help me do this?</u>
6. Now let's make a 4-letter word, **rose**. <u>He gave me a yellow **rose**.</u>
7. Move the letters around and spell **sore**. <u>Have you ever had a **sore** throat?</u>
8. Add 1 letter and spell **shore**. <u>We sat on the **shore** and watched the boats.</u>
9. Now let's spell a 6-letter word, **horses**. <u>**Horses** are strong and beautiful animals.</u>
10. It's secret word time. (Begin with **sh** and end with **s**. We take these to get clean.) <u>After the swim in the pool, everyone took **showers**.</u>

Sort: Have the students sort all the words into rhyming patterns.

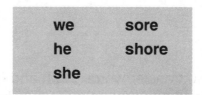

we	sore
he	shore
she	

Transfer: Show the students the two transfer words, **store** and **core**. Say to the students, "Let's pretend we are reading and come to these two new words." Have the students put the new words under the rhyming words and pronounce all the words.

Word Wall: Call out the five words added in lesson 120—**go, get, him, smaller,** and **them**. Have the students chant them, write them, and check them. Have the students write the rhyming words **pet, swim, trim, wet,** and **slim**.

Lesson 122

Letters: e i h l s s t w
Words: his hit sit set wet with wish swish wishes whistles

Make words:

1. Let's start with the 3-letter word, **his**. <u>Tomorrow is **his** birthday.</u>
2. Now let's spell another 3-letter word, **hit**. <u>She **hit** the ball a long way.</u>
3. Change 1 letter and spell **sit**. <u>**Sit** in the rocking chair.</u>
4. Change 1 letter to spell **set**. <u>Who will help me **set** the table?</u>
5. Change 1 letter to spell **wet**. <u>I walked home in the rain and got very **wet**.</u>
6. Use 4 letters to spell **with**. <u>Please come to the movie **with** me.</u>
7. Change 1 letter to spell **wish**. <u>I **wish** I could see that movie again.</u>
8. Add 1 letter to spell **swish**. <u>We **swish** our teeth with water to help prevent cavities.</u>
9. Use 6 letters to spell **wishes**. <u>I will grant you three **wishes**.</u>
10. It's time for the secret word. I will give you a minute and then give you some clues. (Start with **wh** and end with **s**. This is a sound you can make with your mouth.) <u>The boy **whistles** as he walks down the road.</u>

Sort: First, have the students sort out **wish** and **wishes** and use both words in sentences. Next, have the students sort all the words into rhyming patterns.

wish	
wishes	

hit	set	wish
sit	wet	swish

Transfer: Show the students the two transfer words, **dish** and **quit**. Say to the students, "Let's pretend we are reading and come to these two new words." Have the students put the new words under the rhyming words and pronounce all the words.

Word Wall: Call out **scare, skate, smaller, stop,** and **sweater**. Have the students chant, write, and check these words. Tell the students that these words are on the Word Wall to help them remember the sounds for **sc, sk, sm, st,** and **sw**. Say the following words beginning with these letters and ask the students which two letters they would use to begin writing these words: **swell, stack, story, swing, smash,** and **smelly**. Tell the students that because **sc** and **sk** have the same sound, you can't tell which spelling to use by listening.

Lesson 123

Letters: o o o m r r t w
Words: to too two tow mow row moo room motor tomorrow

Make words:

1. Take 2 letters and spell **to**. <u>We are going **to** the game.</u>
2. Add 1 letter to spell the **too** that means **too** big. <u>It is **too** late for TV now.</u>
3. Change 1 letter and spell the number **two**. <u>I have **two** arms.</u>
4. Move the letters and spell **tow**. <u>The **tow** truck came and took the wrecked car away.</u>
5. Change 1 letter to spell **mow**. <u>I like to **mow** the grass.</u>
6. Change 1 letter to spell **row**. <u>Put the chairs in a straight **row**.</u>
7. Let's spell a silly-sounding 3-letter word, **moo**. <u>Cows **moo**.</u>
8. Use 4 letters to spell **room**. <u>This is a nice big **room**.</u>
9. Use 5 letters to spell **motor**. <u>We got a new **motor** so the boat would run better.</u>
10. It's time for the secret word. (Start with **t** and end with **w**. This word means the day after today.) <u>I will see you **tomorrow**.</u>

Sort: First, have the students sort out **to, too,** and **two**, talk about the meanings of each word, and use each word in a sentence. Next, have the students sort all the words into rhyming patterns.

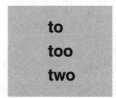

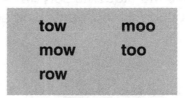

Transfer: Show the students the two transfer words, **glow** and **grow**. Say to the students, "Let's pretend we are reading and come to these two new words." Have the students put the new words under the rhyming words and pronounce all the words.

Word Wall: Teach endings by choosing **smaller, biggest, black, slow,** and **smart**. Have the students chant them, write them, and check them. Tell them the endings **er** and **est** can be added to words to show differences. Use examples from your room to illustrate **small, smaller, smallest** and **big, bigger, biggest**. Have the students notice that the **g** doubles in **biggest** when **est** is added. Have the students spell **blackest, slower, slowest, smarter,** and **smartest**.

Lesson 124

Letters: e i c c h k n

Words: in kin ice nice Nick neck chin chick check chicken

Make words:

1. Let's start with a Word Wall word, **in**.
2. Let's spell a 3-letter word, **kin**. When someone is related to us, we say they are our **kin**.
3. Use 3 letters to spell **ice**. Could I have some **ice** for my drink?
4. Add 1 letter and spell **nice**. You are being very **nice** today.
5. Change 1 letter to spell **Nick**. Santa Claus used to be called Saint **Nick**.
6. Change 1 letter to spell **neck**. A giraffe has a long **neck**.
7. Let's spell one more 4-letter word, **chin**. The pig said, "Not by the hair of my chinny **chin chin**.
8. Use 5 letters to spell **chick**. A baby chicken is called a **chick**.
9. Change 1 letter and spell **check**. Please **check** your words to be sure you have all the letters in the right places.
10. Now it's time for the secret word. I bet someone will get it today. The dog chased after the **chicken**.

Sort: First, have the students sort **chick** and **chicken** and talk about how they are related. Have the students pronounce all the words and sort them into rhyming patterns.

chick
chicken

in	ice	Nick	neck
kin	nice	chick	check
chin			

Transfer: Show the students the two transfer words, **peck** and **brick**. Say to the students, "Let's pretend we are reading and come to these two new words." Have the students put the new words under the rhyming words and pronounce all the words.

Word Wall: Choose five starred words from the Word Wall for review. Have the students chant them, write them, and check them. Say five words that rhyme with and have the same pattern as the Word Wall words and have the students spell these new words.

Lesson 125

Word Wall Words: how nice two who with
Secret Words: showers whistles tomorrow chicken

To review the letters and sounds, the big letters for each secret word are put in the pocket chart and the students are invited to come and make words they remember from each lesson. (Students do not have their little individual letters.) Students should not try to make all the words from each lesson, but do have them make each secret word. Be sure they make the five words that will be added to the Word Wall.

Review:

1. Put the letters **e, o, h, r, s, s,** and **w** in the pocket chart. Let students come and make any words they can. Be sure they make **who** and **how** and show them the Word Wall cards for **who** and **how**.
2. Remove the **o** and **r**. Add **i, l,** and **t**. Again, let students come and make some words. Be sure they make **with** and show them the Word Wall card for **with**.
3. Remove all the letters except **t** and **w**. Add **o, o, o, m, r,** and **r**. Again, let students come and make some words. Be sure they make **two** and show them the Word Wall card for **two**.
4. Remove all the letters. Add the **e, i, c, c, h, k,** and **n**. Again, let students come and make some words. Be sure they make **nice** and show them the Word Wall card for **nice**.

Word Wall:

1. Place the words on the Word Wall, have the students say each word, and use each word in a sentence. Put the number **2** next to the word **two** to distinguish it from **to** and **too**. Review the meanings of **to, too,** and **two** and have the students use **to, too,** and **two** in sentences. Review this idea often in the coming lessons as this is a difficult concept for most students. **How** and **nice** are starred words.
2. Point to each new word and have the students chant its spelling three times in a rhythmic manner.
3. Have the students write each new word as you model good writing using the board or overhead. Model and talk about correct letter formation as you write each word.
4. Have the students check their words by pointing to each letter and saying it aloud. Have them fix any words that need fixing.
5. If possible, give everyone a copy of the Take-Home Word Wall (page 182).

Lessons 126-130
Letters and Sounds: Review

Lesson 126

Letters: a e e h r t w
Words: at hat what were here tree three there where weather

Make words:

1. Take 2 letters and spell **at**.
2. Add 1 letter and spell **hat**.
3. Add 1 letter and spell **what**. <u>**What** would you like for lunch?</u>
4. Let's spell one of our Word Wall words, **were**. <u>We **were** late this morning.</u>
5. Change 1 letter and spell **here**. <u>Please come **here**.</u>
6. Let's spell one more 4-letter word, **tree**. <u>We had a picnic under the **tree**.</u>
7. Add 1 letter to spell **three**. <u>You may have **three** cookies.</u>
8. Move the letters around and spell **there**. <u>I live over **there**.</u>
9. Change 1 letter and spell **where**. <u>**Where** do you live?</u>
10. It's secret word time. (Start with **w** and end with **er**. Think about rain and sun and snow.) <u>We all want to know what the **weather** is going to be.</u>

Sort: Have the students sort all the words into rhyming patterns. Help students notice that **here** and **were** are spelled like **where** and **there**, but they don't rhyme. **What** is spelled like **at** and **hat** but these words don't rhyme

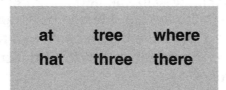

at	tree	where
hat	three	there

Transfer: Show the students the two transfer words, **bee** and **free**. Say to the students, "Let's pretend we are reading and come to these two new words." Have the students put the new words under the rhyming words and pronounce all the words.

Word Wall: Call out the five words added in lesson 125—**how, nice, two, who,** and **with**. Remind the students that **two** is the number **2**. Have the students chant, write, and check the new words. Then, have the students write the rhyming words **rice, chow, slice, ice,** and **price**.

Lesson 127

Letters: e o c d l s t
Words: let lot cot old sold told cold scold oldest coldest

Make words:

1. Let's use 3 letters to spell **let**. <u>I will **let** you use my markers.</u>
2. Change 1 letter and spell **lot**. <u>(Name) reads a **lot** of books.</u>
3. Change 1 letter and spell **cot**. <u>I visited my grandma and slept on a **cot** in the living room.</u>
4. Let's spell one more 3-letter word, **old**. <u>How **old** are you?</u>
5. Add 1 letter and spell **sold**. <u>I **sold** my bike at the yard sale.</u>
6. Change 1 letter and spell **told**. <u>(Name) **told** me a secret.</u>
7. Change 1 letter and spell **cold**. <u>The refrigerator keeps things **cold**.</u>
8. Add 1 letter and spell **scold**. <u>The mother will **scold** her child if she runs into the street.</u>
9. Use 6 letters to spell **oldest**. <u>I am the **oldest** one in my family.</u>
10. It's time for the secret word. I will give you a minute and then give you some clues. (Start with **cold** and add your other letters.) <u>It was the **coldest** day of the whole year.</u>

Sort: First, have the students sort the words **cold** and **coldest** and **old** and **oldest**. Then, have the students use each of these words in a sentence. Finally, have them sort all the words into rhyming patterns.

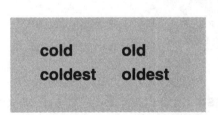

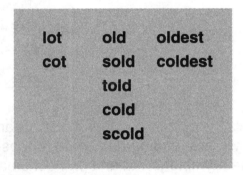

Transfer: Show the students the two transfer words, **gold** and **rot**. Say to the students, "Let's pretend we are reading and come to these two new words." Have the students put the new words under the rhyming words and pronounce all the words.

Word Wall: Call out the often confused words **to, too, two, there,** and **their**. Remind the students of the meanings of these words and use each word in a sentence. Have the students chant them, write them, and check them. Then, say a sentence leaving a blank where one of these words should go. Have the students decide which word would make sense in the sentence and write the word again.

Lesson 128

Letters: a e d h s v
Words: sad had has ash dash have shed shade saved shaved

Make words:

1. Take 3 letters and spell **sad**. <u>Why are you **sad**?</u>
2. Change 1 letter to spell **had**. <u>My cat **had** four kittens.</u>
3. Change 1 letter to spell **has**. <u>One kitten **has** a black tail.</u>
4. Move the letters around to spell **ash**. <u>When wood burns, it turns to **ash**.</u>
5. Add 1 letter to spell **dash**. <u>It was raining hard so we made a **dash** for the car.</u>
6. Let's spell another 4-letter word, **have**. <u>Can we **have** another cookie?</u>
7. Let's spell one more 4-letter word, **shed**. <u>I keep my tools in an old **shed**.</u>
8. Use 5 letters to spell **shade**. <u>I always try to park in the **shade**.</u>
9. Let's spell one more 5-letter word, **saved**. <u>The man jumped into the pool and **saved** the drowning child.</u>
10. It's time for the secret word. (Keep your **saved** and add the **h** someplace.) <u>My uncle **shaved** off his beard.</u>

Sort: Have the students sort all the words into rhyming patterns.

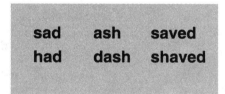

sad	ash	saved
had	dash	shaved

Transfer: Show the students the two transfer words, **cash** and **glad**. Say to the students, "Let's pretend we are reading and come to these two new words." Have the students put the new words under the rhyming words and pronounce all the words.

Word Wall: Call out the often confused words **how, who, two, to,** and **too**. Remind the students of the words' meanings and use each word in a sentence. Have the students chant them, write them, and check them. Then, say a sentence leaving a blank where one of these words should go. Have the students decide which word would make sense in the sentence and write the word again.

Lesson 129

Letters: a e e h l n p s t
Words: pet pest past last east least sheep sleep asleep please elephants

Make words:

1. Let's start with a 3-letter word, **pet**.
2. Add 1 letter and spell **pest**. Don't be such a **pest**!
3. Change 1 letter and spell **past**. She walked **past** my house.
4. Change 1 letter and spell **last**. Who wants to be **last** in line?
5. Change 1 letter and spell **east**. The sun comes up in the **east**.
6. Add 1 letter and spell **least**. At **least** let me look at your new bike.
7. Use 5 letters to spell **sheep**. We saw **sheep** at the petting zoo.
8. Change 1 letter to spell **sleep**. On the weekends, I **sleep** late.
9. Add 1 letter to spell **asleep**. I was fast **asleep** when the phone rang.
10. Move the letters in **asleep** around and spell **please**. **Please** come here.
11. Now it's time for the secret word. It's a hard one, and I will give you some clues. (Start with **e** and end with **s**. Put the **p** and **h** together in the middle. **Ph** has an **f** sound. These are big animals with trunks.) I saw **elephants** at the zoo and at the circus.

Sort: First, have the students sort the words **sleep** and **asleep**. Then, have the students use each of these words in a sentence. Finally, have the students sort all the words into rhyming patterns.

sleep
asleep

past	sleep	east
last	sheep	least
	asleep	

Transfer: Show the students the two transfer words, **steep** and **fast**. Say to the students, "Let's pretend we are reading and come to these two new words." Have the students put the new words under the rhyming words and pronounce all the words.

Word Wall: Choose five starred words from the Word Wall for review. Have the students chant them, write them, and check them. Say five words that rhyme with and have the same pattern as the Word Wall words and have students spell these new words.

Lesson 130

Word Wall Words: have here old what where
Secret Words: weather coldest shaved elephants

To review the letters and sounds, the big letters for each secret word are put in the pocket chart and the students are invited to come and make words they remember from each lesson. (Students do not have their little individual letters.) Students should not try to make all the words from each lesson, but do have them make each secret word. Be sure they make the five words that will be added to the Word Wall.

Review:

1. Put the letters **a, e, e, h, r, t,** and **w** in the pocket chart. Let students come and make any words they can. Be sure they make **here, what,** and **where** and show them the Word Wall cards for **here, what,** and **where**.
2. Remove all the letters except **e** and **t**. Add **o, c, d, l,** and **s**. Again, let students come and make some words. Be sure they make **old** and show them the Word Wall card for **old**.
3. Remove all the letters except **e** and **s**. Add **a, d, h,** and **v**. Again, let students come and make some words. Be sure they make **have** and show them the Word Wall card for **have**.
4. Remove the **d** and **v**. Add the **e, l, n, p,** and **t**. Again, let students come and make some words.

Word Wall:

1. Place the words on the Word Wall, have the students say each word, and use each word in a sentence. **Old** is the only starred word.
2. Point to each new word and have the students chant its spelling three times in a rhythmic manner.
3. Have the students write each new word as you model good writing using the board or overhead. Model and talk about correct letter formation as you write each word.
4. Have the students check their words by pointing to each letter and saying it aloud. Have them fix any words that need fixing.
5. If possible, give everyone a copy of the Take-Home Word Wall (page 183).

Lessons 131-135
Letters and Sounds: Review

Lesson 131

Letters: i o u f m n r s
Words: or our sun run fun for form from sour uniforms

Make words:

1. Let's start with a Word Wall word, **or**.
2. Add 1 letter and spell **our**. <u>This is **our** classroom.</u>
3. Use 3 letters to spell **sun**.
4. Change 1 letter and spell **run**.
5. Change 1 letter and spell **fun**.
6. Let's spell one more Word Wall word, **for**.
7. Add 1 letter to **for** and spell **form**. <u>I have to fill out this **form** and send it to the office.</u>
8. Move the letters and spell **from**. <u>What country is she **from**?</u>
9. Start over and use 4 letters to spell **sour**. <u>Milk tastes awful when it is **sour**.</u>
10. It's secret word time. (Begin with **u** and end with **s**. These are a type of clothes people wear. Policemen wear them. Baseball players wear them. Marching bands wear them, too.) <u>Do you like the band's new **uniforms**?</u>

Sort: Have the students sort all the words into rhyming patterns.

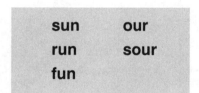

sun	our
run	sour
fun	

Transfer: Show the students the two transfer words, **flour** and **stun**. Say to the students, "Let's pretend we are reading and come to these two new words." Have the students put the new words under the rhyming words and pronounce all the words.

Word Wall: Call out the five words added in lesson 130—**have, here, old, what,** and **where**. Have the students chant them, write them, and check them. Have students spell the following words that rhyme with **old**: **gold, cold, told, hold,** and **scold**.

Lesson 132

Letters: a i g h h s w y
Words: hi was saw shy why say way sway high wish highways

Make words:

1. Use 2 letters and spell **hi**. <u>When we see our friends, we say, "**Hi.**"</u>
2. Spell the Word Wall word, **was**.
3. Move the letters around to spell another Word Wall word, **saw**.
4. Use 3 letters to spell **shy**. <u>Do you ever feel **shy** when you meet new people?</u>
5. Change 1 letter to spell **why**. <u>**Why** do you feel shy?</u>
6. Use 3 letters to spell **say**. <u>What did you **say**?</u>
7. Change 1 letter to spell **way**. <u>That box is in my **way**.</u>
8. Add 1 letter to spell **sway**. <u>Did you ever see the trees **sway** in the wind?</u>
9. Use 4 letters to spell another **high**. <u>I can't reach that **high**.</u> This **high** uses 2 letters you don't hear, just like the Word Wall word, **night**.
10. Let's spell one more 4-letter word, **wish**. <u>I **wish** all my students were as quick and smart as you are.</u>
11. It's time for the secret word. I will give you a minute, and then give you some clues. (Start with the **high** that means tall and add another word you made.) <u>We drove on many **highways** when we took our long trip.</u>

Sort: First, have the students sort out the words **high, way,** and **highways**. Have them notice that **highways** is a compound word with **high, way,** and **s**. Finally, have the students sort all the words into rhyming patterns.

high		shy	say
way		why	way
highways			sway

Transfer: Show the students the two transfer words, **try** and **stray**. Say to the students, "Let's pretend we are reading and come to these two new words." Have the students put the new words under the rhyming words and pronounce all the words.

Word Wall: Review word endings by choosing **nice, old, scare, sweater,** and **want**. Have the students chant these words, write them, and check them. Then, have the students spell **wanting, scared, older, nicest,** and **sweaters**.

Lesson 133

Letters: e o c m s t
Words: to so me met set cot most some come comets

Make words:

1. Let's start with the Word Wall word, **to**. <u>We went **to** McDonald's®.</u>
2. Let's spell another Word Wall word, **so**.
3. Let's spell one more Word Wall word, **me**.
4. Add 1 letter to spell **met**. <u>I **met** her at a birthday party.</u>
5. Change 1 letter to spell **set**. <u>She bought a new **set** of dishes.</u>
6. Let's spell one more 3-letter word, **cot**. <u>I slept on the **cot**.</u>
7. Use 4 letters to spell **most**. <u>I have the **most** beautiful cat.</u>
8. Let's spell the Word Wall word, **some**.
9. Change 1 letter to spell **come**. <u>Can I **come** with you?</u>
10. It's time for the secret word. (Start with **come** and add your remaining letters to spell something that is out in space.) <u>**Comets** whirl around in outer space.</u>

Sort: Have the students sort all the words into rhyming patterns.

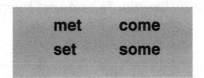

met	come
set	some

Transfer: Show the students the two transfer words, **bet** and **wet**. Say to the students, "Let's pretend we are reading and come to these two new words." Have the students put the new words under the rhyming words and pronounce all the words.

Word Wall: Call out the often confused words **have, here, her, him,** and **has**. Remind students of the words' meanings and use each word in a sentence. Have the students chant these words, write them, and check them. Then, say a sentence leaving a blank where one of these words should go. Have the students decide which word would make sense in the sentence and write each word again.

Lesson 134

Letters: i o l l p s w
Words: oil owl low slow will pill soil spoil spill pillows

Make words:

1. Let's start with a Word Wall word, **oil**.
2. Change 1 letter to spell **owl**. The **owl** flies around at night and sleeps during the day.
3. Move the letters and spell **low**. When it hasn't rained in awhile, the water level in the creeks and rivers is **low**.
4. Add 1 letter and spell **slow**. We don't have any **slow** word makers in here.
5. Use four letters to spell **will**. I **will** help you if you need help.
6. Change 1 letter to spell **pill**. She took a **pill** because she had a headache.
7. Let's spell one more 4-letter word, **soil**. **Soil** is another word for dirt.
8. Add 1 letter to **soil** and spell **spoil**. When I was little, my grandma used to **spoil** me.
9. Use five letters to spell **spill**. If you **spill** something, just wipe it up.
10. Now it's time for the secret word. (Start with **pill** and add the other letters to make something you lie your head on when you sleep.) I have two **pillows** on my bed.

Sort: Have the students pronounce all the words and sort them into rhyming patterns.

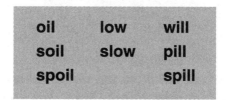

oil	low	will
soil	slow	pill
spoil		spill

Transfer: Show the students the two transfer words, **broil** and **grow**. Say to the students, "Let's pretend we are reading and come to these two new words." Have the students put the new words under the rhyming words and pronounce all the words.

Word Wall: Choose five starred words from the Word Wall for review. Have the students chant them, write them, and check them. Say five words that rhyme with and have the same patterns as the Word Wall words and have the students spell these new words.

Lesson 135

Word Wall Words: come from our will why
Secret Words: uniforms highways comets pillows

To review the letters and sounds, the big letters for each secret word are put in the pocket chart and the students are invited to come and make words they remember from each lesson. (Students do not have their little individual letters.) Students should not try to make all the words from each lesson, but do have them make each secret word. Be sure they make the five words that will be added to the Word Wall.

Review:

1. Put the letters **i, o, u, f, m, n, r,** and **s** in the pocket chart. Let students come and make any words they can. Be sure they make **from** and **our** and show them the Word Wall cards for **from** and **our**.
2. Remove all the letters except **i** and **s**. Add **a, g, h, h, w,** and **y**. Again, let students come and make some words. Be sure they make **why** and show them the Word Wall card for **why**.
3. Remove all the letters except **s**. Add the **e, o, c, m,** and **t**. Again, let students come and make some words. Be sure they make **come** and show them the Word Wall card for **come**.
4. Remove all the letters except **o** and **s**. Add the **i, l, l, p,** and **w**. Again, let students come and make some words. Be sure they make **will** and show them the Word Wall card for **will**.

Word Wall:

1. Place the words on the Word Wall, have the students say each word, and use each word in a sentence. **Will** and **why** are starred words
2. Point to each new word and have the students chant its spelling three times in a rhythmic manner.
3. Have the students write each new word as you model good writing using the board or overhead. Model and talk about correct letter formation as you write each word.
4. Have the students check their words by pointing to each letter and saying it aloud. Have them fix any words that need fixing.
5. If possible, give everyone a copy of the Take-Home Word Wall (page 184).

Lesson 136

Letters: e n t t w y
Words: we wet net yet ten new newt went tent twenty

Make words:

1. Take 2 letters and spell **we**. <u>We are making words.</u>
2. Add just 1 letter and spell **wet**. <u>I got **wet** walking here in the rain.</u>
3. Change 1 letter and spell **net**. <u>The tennis player hit the ball over the **net**.</u>
4. Change 1 letter and spell **yet**. <u>Lunch is not ready **yet**.</u>
5. Use 3 letters to spell **ten**. <u>She is **ten** years old.</u>
6. Let's spell a Word Wall word, **new**.
7. Add 1 letter to **new** to spell **newt**. <u>A **newt** looks like a frog with a tail.</u>
8. Move the letters in **newt** and spell **went**. <u>(NAME) **went** to the hospital.</u>
9. Change 1 letter and spell **tent**. <u>We sleep in a **tent** when we camp out.</u>
10. It's secret word time. (Start with **tw**. Add your other letters to spell a number.) <u>Ten plus ten equals **twenty**.</u>

Sort: Have the students sort all the words into rhyming patterns.

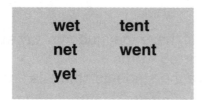

wet	tent
net	went
yet	

Transfer: Show the students the two transfer words, **spent** and **lent**. Say to the students, "Let's pretend we are reading and come to these two new words." Have the students put the new words under the rhyming words and pronounce all the words.

Word Wall: Call out the five words added in lesson 135—**come, from, our, will,** and **why**. Have the students chant them, write them, and check them. Have the students spell the rhyming words **fill, spill, hill, chill,** and **thrill**.

Lesson 137

Letters: a e e h r t t
Words: at hat rat the ate rate that here there three teeth theater

Make words:

1. Let's start with the Word Wall word, **at**.
2. Add 1 letter and spell **hat**.
3. Change 1 letter and spell **rat**.
4. Let's spell another Word Wall word, **the**.
5. Let's spell one more 3-letter word, **ate**. <u>We **ate** breakfast.</u>
6. Add 1 letter and spell **rate**. <u>How would you **rate** that team?</u>
7. Use 4 letters to spell **that**. <u>**That** is my book.</u>
8. Spell the Word Wall word, **here**. <u>(NAME) is right **here**.</u>
9. Add 1 letter to spell the Word Wall word, **there**. <u>(NAME) is over **there**.</u>
10. Move the letters around to spell **three**. <u>You can each have **three** cookies.</u>
11. Use 5 letters to spell **teeth**. <u>We brush our **teeth** to prevent cavities.</u>
12. It's time for the secret word. I will give you a minute, and then give you some clues. (Start with **th** and end with **er**. This is a place where you can see a movie or a play.) <u>We went to the **theater** on Saturday.</u>

Sort: Have the students sort all the words into rhyming patterns. Help them to notice that **here** and **there** have the same spelling pattern, but do not rhyme.

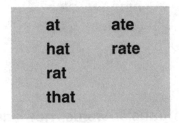

at	ate
hat	rate
rat	
that	

Transfer: Show the students the two transfer words, **chat** and **date**. Say to the students, "Let's pretend we are reading and come to these two new words." Have the students put the new words under the rhyming words and pronounce all the words.

Word Wall: Call out the often confused words **from, for, of, our,** and **are**. Remind the students of the words' meanings and use each word in a sentence. Have the students chant them, write them, and check them. Then, say a sentence leaving a blank where one of the words should go. Have the students decide which word would make sense in the sentence and write the word again.

Lesson 138

Letters: e i c k l n s
Words: ski ice nice like skin neck Nick sick lick slick slice nickels

Make words:

1. Take 3 letters and spell **ski**. <u>Can you **ski**?</u>
2. Use 3 letters to spell **ice**. <u>I slipped and fell on the **ice**.</u>
3. Add 1 letter to spell **nice**. <u>(NAME) is a very **nice** person.</u>
4. Let's spell another 4-letter word, **like**. <u>What do you **like** to eat?</u>
5. Use 4 letters to spell **skin**. <u>The baby's **skin** was very soft.</u>
6. Let's spell another 4-letter word, **neck**. <u>Sometimes I get a stiff **neck**.</u>
7. Change 1 letter and spell **Nick**. <u>**Nick** works at the grocery store.</u>
8. Change 1 letter and you can spell **sick**. <u>No one likes to be **sick**.</u>
9. Change 1 letter and spell **lick**. <u>I like to **lick** lollipops.</u>
10. Add 1 letter and spell **slick**. <u>The roads were **slick** during the snowstorm.</u>
11. Change 1 letter and spell **slice**. <u>You may have another **slice** of pie.</u>
12. It's time for the secret word. If you need them, I will give you some clues. (Start with an **n** and end with **s**. These are coins worth five cents.) <u>Five **nickels** is 25 cents.</u>

Sort: Have the students sort all the words into rhyming patterns.

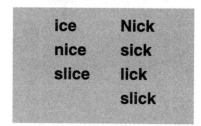

ice	Nick
nice	sick
slice	lick
	slick

Transfer: Show the students the two transfer words, **rice** and **brick**. Say to the students, "Let's pretend we are reading and come to these two new words." Have the students put the new words under the rhyming words and pronounce all the words.

Word Wall: Call out the often confused words **there, their, they, them,** and **then**. Remind the students of the words' meanings and use each word in a sentence. Have the students chant them, write them, and check them. Then, say a sentence leaving a blank where one of these words should go. Have the students decide which word would make sense in the sentence and write the word again.

Lesson 139

Letters: e o o u d g h s
Words: us use Sue due dug hug dog good hose house doghouse

Make words:

1. Let's start with a Word Wall word, **us**.
2. Add 1 letter and spell another Word Wall word, **use**.
3. Move the letters around and spell the name, **Sue**.
4. Change 1 letter and spell **due**. <u>These books are **due** back at the library today.</u>
5. Change 1 letter and spell **dug**. <u>We **dug** a big hole and planted a tree.</u>
6. Change 1 letter and spell **hug**. <u>The boy gave his grandma a big **hug**.</u>
7. Let's spell one more 3-letter word, **dog**. <u>Do you have a **dog**?</u>
8. Let's spell a 4-letter word, **good**. <u>Was that a **good** book?</u>
9. Let's spell another 4-letter word, **hose**. <u>We used the **hose** to wash the car.</u>
10. Add one letter to **hose** to spell **house**. <u>I live in a little, yellow **house**.</u>
11. Now it's time for the secret word. (It's a compound word that uses two of the words you made. You might have one if you have a dog.) <u>My dog sleeps in her **doghouse**.</u>

Sort: First, have the students sort **house**, **dog**, and **doghouse**. Next, have the students sort all the words into rhyming patterns.

dog		due	dug
house		Sue	hug
doghouse			

Transfer: Show the students the two transfer words, **plug** and **true**. Say to the students, "Let's pretend we are reading and come to these two new words." Have the students put the new words under the rhyming words and pronounce all the words.

Word Wall: Choose five starred words from the Word Wall for review. Have the students chant them, write them, and check them. Say five words that rhyme with and have the same patterns as the Word Wall words and have the students spell these new words.

Lesson 140

Word Wall Words: good like that we went
Secret Words: twenty theater nickels doghouse

To review the letters and sounds, the big letters for each secret word are put in the pocket chart and the students are invited to come and make words they remember from each lesson. (Students do not have their little individual letters.) Students should not try to make all the words from each lesson, but do have them make each secret word. Be sure they make the five words that will be added to the Word Wall.

Review:

1. Put the letters **e, n, t, t, w,** and **y** in the pocket chart. Let students come and make any words they can. Be sure they make **we** and **went** and show them the Word Wall cards for **we** and **went**.
2. Remove the **n, w,** and **y**. Add **a, e, h,** and **r**. Again, let students come and make some words. Be sure they make **that** and show them the Word Wall card for **that**.
3. Remove all the letters except **e**. Add **i, c, k, l, n,** and **s**. Again, let students come and make some words. Be sure they make **like** and show them the Word Wall card for **like**.
4. Remove all the letters except **s**. Add the **e, o, o, u, d, g,** and **h**. Again, let students come and make some words. Be sure they make **good** and show them the Word Wall card for **good**.

Word Wall:

1. Place the words on the Word Wall, have the students say each word, and use each word in a sentence. **Like, that,** and **went** are starred words.
2. Point to each new word and have the students chant its spelling three times in a rhythmic manner.
3. Have the students write each new word as you model good writing using the board or overhead. Model and talk about correct letter formation as you write each word.
4. Have the students check their words by pointing to each letter and saying it aloud. Have them fix any words that need fixing.
5. If possible, give everyone a copy of the Take-Home Word Wall (page 185).

Systematic Sequential Phonics They Use
Review Activities

These review activities can be done when all the lessons are completed or whenever you feel the need and have the time to review important concepts. The examples include all 140 Word Wall words. If you use these activities before you have all the words on the Word Wall, adjust the activity for the words currently on the wall.

Review Beginning Sounds

The Word Wall contains key words for all the common beginning sounds—single consonants, digraphs (**sh, ch, th,** and **wh**), blends (**br, bl, st,** etc.), the **s** sound of **c**, the **j** sound of **g**, and **qu**. You can call out these words and have the students write them to review the beginning sounds. Tell the students that when they are reading and come to a word they don't know, these key words can help them with the beginning sounds.

Single Consonants

b because before best big biggest boy but

c can car come could

d day do

f for

g get girl go good

h had has have he her here him how hurt

j jump jumping

k kittens

l like little look

m make me more my

n new nice night no not now

p pet

r rain red ride run

s said same saw see six so some

t to too tell

v very

w walk want was we went were will with

y you your

z zoo

Blends

bl black

br brother

cl cloud

cr creatures

dr dry

fl float

fr friend from

gl glad

gr green

pl player

pr probably

sc scare

sk skate

sl slow

sm smart smaller

sn snake

sp sport

st stop stopped

sw sweater

tr train

Digraphs		**C (S); G (J); Qu**	
ch	children	c (s)	centers
sh	she	g (j)	gym
th	that the their them then there they things this those	qu	question
wh	what when where why		

Vowel Patterns

The Word Wall contains key word examples for all the common vowel patterns. Call out these words and have the students write them to review the vowel patterns. Tell the students that when they are reading and come to a word they don't know, these key words can help them with the vowel sounds. Remember that vowels are pronounced differently in different parts of the country. If your students do not pronounce these words with the given sound, do not use them as examples for that sound. Below are key words from the Word Wall words for each vowel sound. (Words listed in two places represent two vowel patterns.)

a	(as in **at**)	after am an and as at black can glad had has that
e	(as in **end**)	biggest centers children get kittens pet question red tell them then went when
i	(as in **it**)	big biggest children him if in is it kittens little six this will with
o	(as in **on**)	not on stop stopped
u	(as in **up**)	but jump jumping run under up us
a	(as in **make, rain,** and **day**)	day make player rain same skate snake train
e	(as in **eat, see,** and **he**)	creatures eat green he me see she we
i	(as in **ride, night,** and **I**)	I like nice night ride
o	(as in **those, float,** and **no**)	float go no old over so those
u	(as in **use**)	use
ar	(as in **smart**)	car smart
or	(as in **for**)	for more or sport
er	(as in **her**)	after brother centers her over player
ir	(as in **girl**)	girl
ur	(as in **hurt**)	hurt
aw	(as in **saw**)	saw
al	(as in **walk**)	all smaller walk
au	(as in **because**)	because
ou	(as in **cloud**)	cloud our

ow	(as in **now**)	how now
ow	(as in **slow**)	slow
oi	(as in **oil**)	oil
oy	(as in **boy**)	boy
oo	(as in **zoo**)	too zoo
oo	(as in **look**)	good look
ew	(as in **new**)	new
y	(as in **my**)	dry my why
y	(as in **very**)	probably very

Rhyming Patterns

The Word Wall contains key word examples for many common rhyming patterns. These words are starred on the Word Wall. Call out some of the starred words and have the students write them. Then, make up a sentence containing a rhyming word and have the students use the correct starred word to spell the rhyming word.

all*   ball call fall hall mall tall wall small stall

am*   ham jam Pam ram Sam clam cram slam

an*   ban can Dan fan man pan ran tan van bran clan plan scan than

and*   band hand land sand brand gland grand stand

at*   bat cat fat hat mat Pat rat sat brat chat flat scat that

big*   dig fig jig pig rig wig twig

black*   back hack Jack lack Mack pack quack rack sack tack crack shack slack smack snack stack track

boy*   joy Roy soy toy Troy

but*   cut gut hut jut nut rut shut strut

can*   (an)

car*   bar far jar tar scar star

day*   bay hay Jay lay may pay Ray say way clay gray play pray spray stay stray sway tray

dry*   by my cry fly fry pry shy sky sly spy try why

eat*   beat heat meat neat seat cheat treat wheat

end*   bend lend mend send tend blend spend trend

float*   boat coat goat moat gloat throat

get*   bet jet let met net pet set wet yet fret

glad*   bad dad fad had mad pad sad Brad Chad

had*   (glad)

him*   dim Jim Kim rim Tim brim grim slim swim trim whim

how*   bow cow now vow brow chow plow

in*   bin fin kin pin tin win chin grin skin spin thin twin

it*   bit fit hit kit lit pit quit sit grit skit slit spit split

jump* bump dump hump lump pump clump grump plump slump stump thump

like* bike hike Mike spike strike

look* book cook hook nook took brook crook shook

make* bake cake fake Jake lake make quake rake take wake brake flake shake snake

more* bore core sore tore wore chore score shore snore store

my*   (dry)

new*   few blew chew crew drew flew grew stew

nice* ice dice lice mice rice price slice spice twice

night* light might right sight tight bright flight fright slight

not*   cot dot got hot lot pot rot clot plot shot slot spot trot

now*   (how)

oil*   boil coil foil soil broil spoil

old*   bold cold fold gold hold mold sold told scold

pet*   (get)

rain* main pain brain chain drain grain plain Spain sprain stain strain train

red*   Ed bed fed led Ned Ted wed fled Fred shed shred sled

ride* hide side tide wide bride glide pride slide

run*   bun fun sun spun stun

same* came fame game lame name tame blame flame frame shame

saw*   jaw law paw raw claw draw slaw straw

see*   bee fee flee free glee tree

skate* ate date gate hate Kate late mate rate crate plate state

slow* bow low mow row tow blow crow flow glow grow show snow

smart* art Bart cart dart mart part chart start

snake* (make)

stop* bop cop hop mop pop top chop crop drop flop plop prop shop

tell* bell fell sell well yell shell smell spell swell

that* (at)

then* Ben den hen Ken men pen ten when

things* kings rings sings wings brings clings flings slings springs stings strings swings

those* hose nose pose rose chose close

train* (rain)

went* bent dent lent rent sent tent vent spent

when* (then)

why*   (dry)

will* ill bill dill fill gill hill Jill kill mill pill till chill drill grill skill spill still thrill

Common Endings

The Word Wall has a key word for the common endings **s, ed, ing, er (person or thing), er (more),** **est (most), and ly**. These key words are:

centers, kittens, things, creatures	**s**
stopped (double p)	**ed**
jumping	**ing**
player	**er (person)**
smaller	**er (more)**
biggest (double g)	**est (most)**
probably	**ly**

Here are the Word Wall words to which those endings can be added to spell new words:

big	bigger	**make**	makes making maker makers
black	blacker blackest	**new**	newer newest
boy	boys	**nice**	nicer nicest nicely
brother	brothers brotherly	**night**	nights
car	cars	**oil**	oils oiled oiling
cloud	clouds	**old**	older oldest
come	comes coming	**pet**	pets petted petting
day	days	**player**	players
dry	dries dried drying dryer	**question**	questions questioned questioning questioner questioners
eat	eats eating eater eaters	**rain**	rains rained raining
end	ends ended ending endings	**red**	redder reddest
float	floats floated floating	**ride**	rides riding rider riders
friend	friends friendly friendlier friendliest	**run**	runs running runner runners
get	gets getting	**scare**	scares scared scaring
girl	girl	**skate**	skates skated skating skater skaters
glad	gladly	**slow**	slower slowest slowly
green	greener greenest	**smart**	smarter smartest
gym	gyms	**snake**	snakes
hurt	hurts hurting	**sport**	sports
jump	jumps jumped jumper jumpers	**stop**	stops stopping stopper
like	likes liked liking likely	**sweater**	sweaters
little	littler littlest	**tell**	tells telling teller
look	looks looked looking		

train	trains trained training trainer trainers	**want**	wants wanted wanting
use	uses used using user users	**will**	willing
walk	walks walked walking walker walkers	**zoo**	zoos

Sentences Using Names and Word Wall Words

Students love to write about themselves and each other. Dictate a few sentences to the students and have them write the sentences. After they write the sentences, have the students check them with you, noting capital letters and punctuation. Use endings you have taught and discuss spelling changes as needed. Here are a few examples to get you going:

(NAME) saw a big black snake.

(NAME) is a good sport.

(NAME) has a red sweater.

Where is (NAME)?

(NAME) has a little brother.

(NAME) and (NAME) are friends.

(NAME) is very smart.

Will you play with (NAME)?

I want (NAME) to come over here.

(NAME) likes to go to centers.

Is (NAME) in the gym?

(NAME) has a question.

Could (NAME) see the kittens?

Is (NAME) going to walk or ride?

Will (NAME) come on the train?

(NAME) has a new red sweater.

(NAME) has a question.

(NAME) likes to look at the clouds.

(NAME) and (NAME) are good players.

(NAME) is glad because she can skate.

(NAME) and (NAME) do not want it to rain.

The creatures will not scare (NAME).

(NAME) is getting two new kittens.

(NAME) has six brothers.

Skating is a sport (NAME) is very good at.

Be a Mind Reader

Be a Mind Reader is a favorite Word Wall review activity. In this game, the teacher thinks of a word on the Word Wall and then gives five clues to that word. Choose a word and write it on a scrap of paper, but do not let the students see which word you have written. Have students number their papers from one to five, and tell them that you are going to see who can read your mind and figure out which of the Word Wall words you have written on your paper. Tell them you will give them five clues. By the fifth clue, everyone should guess your word, but if they read your mind they might get it before the fifth clue.

For your first clue, try to tell the students something that will narrow down their choices to words which begin with one to three letters. ("It is a word that begins with **a, b,** or **c.**") If you don't have many words on the Word Wall, you can say, "It's one of our Word Wall words," for your first clue. Clues may include any features of the word you want the students to notice ("It has more than two letters." "It has less than four letters." "It has an **e.**" "It does not have a **t.**") Each succeeding clue should narrow down what the word can be until by clue five, there is only one possible word. As you give each clue, students write the word they believe the chosen word to be next to each number. If a new clue fits the word a student has written for a previous clue, the student writes that word again by the next number. When you give clue five, try to have narrowed it down to only two choices. After you have given the fifth and final clue, show the students the word you wrote on your scratch paper and say, "I know you all have the word next to number five, but who has it next to number four? Three? Two? One?" Usually, someone will have guessed it on the first or second clue. Express amazement that they "read your mind!" Here are a few examples to get you started. You can do this activity with any of the Word Wall words.

1. It's one of the Word Wall words that begins with **t**.
2. It begins with **th**.
3. It has five letters.
4. It ends with the letter **e**.
5. It is the **there** that we use when we say something is over **there**.

1. It's one of the Word Wall words that begins with **w, y,** or **z**.
2. It has three letters.
3. It has an **o**.
4. It does not have two **o**'s.
5. It begins with a **y**.

1. It's one of the Word Wall words that begins with **f, g,** or **h**.
2. It has four letters.
3. It does not have two of any letter.
4. It begins with a **g**.
5. It's a word that means happy.

1. It's one of the Word Wall words that begins with **a, b,** or **c**.
2. It has five or more letters.
3. It begins with a **b**.
4. It does not have an **r**.
5. It is a color word.

WORDO

WORDO is a variation of the ever-popular Bingo game. Students love it and don't know they are getting a lot of practice reading and writing words! All you need to play WORDO are some sheets of paper on which 25 blocks have been drawn in, and some small pieces of paper, or objects, for students to use to cover words as they fill in the blocks. You can make your own WORDO sheets, or copy the reproducible WORDO sheet on page 187.

You can use WORDO to review any words, but it is particularly helpful for reviewing those easily confused words such as **were/where, them/then/they,** or **of/for/from.** It is also helpful to review a particular type of word—compound words, names that need capital letters, etc. For each WORDO game, we show the students 24 words (the center space is FREE), which they write in the blank blocks, one word for each blank block. Make sure everyone understands that unlike its Bingo counterpart, all the students will ultimately have all the same words that are called out. Since the students will have written them in different places, however, there will still be winners. (Unfortunately, you can't play for a full card!)

When all the students have filled up their sheets using the 24 words you called out, it is time to play. Shuffle your cards and call out the words, one at a time. Have the students chant the spelling of each word and then cover it on their WORDO sheets using paper squares or small objects. The first student to have a complete row of covered words wins WORDO. Be sure to have the winner tell you the words they have covered, while you check to see that the words have been called. You should also check the winner's sheet to make sure they have the words spelled correctly. If a student has misspelled a word on his WORDO sheet, he cannot win and play continues. Students soon learn to look carefully at each word card you show them, so that they can write it correctly on their sheets. When you have a winner, students can clear their sheets and play again. Here are some possible WORDO lists. Except for the last activity, these WORDO lists use words from the Total Word List (pages 188-190) and not just the Word Wall list.

Compound Words: (Combine cards (**base/ball, night/gown,** etc.) to make 24 words.)

baseball blackbirds bluebirds bookshelf butterfly doghouse downstairs everybody everything football grandchild highways into nightgown peanuts playground raindrops sixteen snowball snowflakes snowplow something strawberry yourself

Words with **s** Ending: (Choose 24 words.)

arms bats blackbirds bluebirds boats brides brothers carrots centers characters comets commutes crawls creatures dancers dens elephants fathers fits fleas friends gifts hands highways horses hundreds jugs jungles kittens legs mothers names nickels notes oats painters parents parrots peanuts pillows players pockets ponds rabbits raindrops showers snowflakes things trains trunks uniforms valentines whistles wigs wings

Words with **ed, ing, est, er, ly,** and **y** Endings: (Choose 24 words.)

biggest camping chewing clapping coldest escaped floating friendly growling hopped hurting jumping mooing oldest player scared shaved shopped skater skinny smaller smallest stopped sweaty teacher walking waved zooming

Words beginning with **bl, br, dr,** and **tr:** (Choose 24 words.)

black blackbirds blast bled blue bluebirds blur Brad brain brat brew bribe brick bride brides bridle brisk broil brother brothers bruise drain draw drip drop drown dry trace track trade train trains tray treasure tree trees trick Troy true trunk trunks trust try

Words beginning with **cl, cr, gl,** and **gr:** (Choose 24 words.)

clan clap clapping claw cling clip cloud clouds clover crash crate crater crawl crawls create creatures crust glad gland glory glow grad grain grand grandchild green greet grin grind groan group grow growl growling grunt

Words beginning with **fl, fr, pl,** and **pr:** (Choose 24 words.)

flake fleas fled flew float floating floss flour flow flu flute fly Fred free fried friend friendly friends fright frighten frog from fry plain plan play player players playground please plow plug pray present pride pro probably proud prowl pry

Words beginning with **sc, sk, sl,** and **sw:** (Choose 24 words.)

scar scare scared scat scold screen skate skater ski skin skinny sky slack slaw sled sleep slice slick slid slide slow slug sly sway sweat sweater sweaty sweep sweet swing swish

Words beginning with **sm, sn,** and **sp:** (Choose 24 words.)

small smaller smallest smart smear smell smother snake snap sneak snip snow snowball snowflakes snowplow Spain speck speed spend spent spider spill spin spoil spoon sport spot sprain spray spree

Words beginning with **st:** (Choose 24 words.)

stab stain stall stamp stand star stare start stay steady steep steer step stew sting stink stir stone stop stopped store strain straw strawberry stray string stun

Words beginning with **ch** and **th:** (Choose 24 words.)

chain chart chase chat cheat check chest chew chewing chick chicken child children chin chose that the theater their them then there they thin thing things think this those three throat

Words beginning with **sh** and **wh:**

shade shaved she shed sheep shelf shell shine ship shook shop shopped shore short shot show showers shut shy what when where whistles why

Easily confused or Tricky Word Wall Words: (Choose 24 words from this list or use other Word Wall words that confuse your students. Be sure to give sentence clues for all the words, especially **to/too/two** and **their/there**.)

are because before centers children come could creatures for friend from gym her here how little nice night of oil our probably question said saw some stopped their them then there they those to too two want was went were what when where who why will with

Take-Home Word Wall
After Lesson 5

A a	I i	S s
at* and* am*		
B b	J j	
	K k	T t
C c	L l	
	M m	
D d	N n	
E e		U u
F f	O o	
		V v
G g		W w
	P p	
	Q q	
H h	R r	X x Y y Z z
had* has		

Take-Home Word Wall
After Lesson 10

A a	I i	S s
at* and* am*	if it* in* is	
B b	**J j**	
	K k	**T t**
C c can*	**L l**	
	M m	
D d	**N n**	
E e		**U u**
F f	**O o**	
		V v
G g		**W w**
	P p	
	Q q	
H h had* has	**R r**	**X x Y y Z z**

Take-Home Word Wall
After Lesson 15

A a
at*
and*
am*

B b

C c
can*

D d

E e

F f

G g

H h
had*
has

I i
if   it*
in*
is

J j
jump*   jumping

K k

L l

M m

N n

O o

P p

Q q

R r
run*

S s

T t

U u
up
us

V v

W w

X x   Y y   Z z

Take-Home Word Wall
After Lesson 20

A a
at*
and*
am*

B b
big*
biggest

C c
can*

D d

E e
end*

F f

G g

H h
had*
has

I i
if   it*
in*
is

J j
jump*   jumping

K k
kittens

L l

M m

N n

O o

P p
pet*

Q q

R r
run*

S s

T t

U u
up
us

V v

W w

X x   Y y   Z z

Take-Home Word Wall
After Lesson 25

A a
at*
and*
am*

B b
big*
biggest

C c
can*

D d

E e
end*

F f

G g

H h
had*
has

I i
if   it*
in*
is

J j
jump*   jumping

K k
kittens

L l

M m

N n
no

O o
on

P p
pet*

Q q

R r
run*

S s
so
stop*
stopped

T t

U u
up
us

V v

W w

X x   Y y   Z z

Take-Home Word Wall
After Lesson 30

A a
at*
and*
am*

B b
big*
biggest

C c
can*
children

D d

E e
end*

F f

G g

H h
had*
has
he

I i
if   it*
in*
is

J j
jump*   jumping

K k
kittens

L l

M m

N n
no

O o
on

P p
pet*

Q q

R r
run*

S s
so
stop*
stopped
she

T t
things*
this

U u
up
us

V v

W w

X x   Y y   Z z

Take-Home Word Wall
After Lesson 35

A a
at* as
and*
am*

B b
big*
biggest

C c
can*
children

D d

E e
end*

F f

G g

H h
had*
has
he

I i
if   it*
in*
is

J j
jump*   jumping

K k
kittens

L l

M m
make*
me

N n
no

O o
on

P p
pet*

Q q

R r
run*

S s
so
stop*
stopped
she
same*
skate*

T t
things*
this

U u
up
us

V v

W w

X x   Y y   Z z

Take-Home Word Wall
After Lesson 40

A a
at*   as
and*
am*

B b
big*
biggest
be

C c
can*
children

D d

E e
end*

F f
friend

G g

H h
had*
has
he

I i
if   it*
in*
is

J j
jump*   jumping

K k
kittens

L l

M m
make*
me

N n
no
night*

O o
on

P p
pet*

Q q

R r
run*
red*
ride*

S s
so
stop*
stopped
she
same*
skate*

T t
things*
this

U u
up
us

V v

W w

X x   Y y   Z z

Take-Home Word Wall
After Lesson 45

A a
at*   as
and*
am*

B b
big*   brother
biggest
be

C c
can*
children

D d

E e
end*

F f
friend

G g

H h
had*
has
he

I i
if   it*
in*
is

J j
jump*   jumping

K k
kittens

L l

M m
make*
me

N n
no
night*

O o
on

P p
pet*

Q q

R r
run*
red*
ride*

S s
so
stop*
stopped
she
same*
skate*

T t
things*
this
to
those*

U u
up   under
us   use

V v

W w

X x   Y y   Z z

Take-Home Word Wall
After Lesson 50

A a
at*   as
and*
am*

B b
big*   brother
biggest
be

C c
can*
children

D d
day*

E e
end*

F f
friend

G g

H h
had*
has
he

I i
if   it*
in*   I
is

J j
jump*   jumping

K k
kittens

L l

M m
make*
me

N n
no
night*

O o
on

P p
pet*   player

Q q

R r
run*   ride*
red*   rain*

S s
so
stop*
stopped
she
same*
skate*

T t
things*
this
to
those*
train*

U u
up   under
us   use

V v

W w

X x   Y y   Z z

Take-Home Word Wall
After Lesson 55

A a
at*   as
and*   an*
am*

B b
big*   brother
biggest
be

C c
can*
children

D d
day*

E e
end*   eat*

F f
friend

G g

H h
had*
has
he

I i
if   it*
in*   I
is

J j
jump*   jumping

K k
kittens

L l

M m
make*
me

N n
no
night*

O o
on

P p
pet*   player

Q q

R r
run*   ride*
red*   rain*

S s
so   see*
stop*
stopped
she
same*
skate*

T t
things*
this
to
those*
train*
the
there

U u
up   under
us   use

V v

W w

X x   Y y   Z z

Take-Home Word Wall
After Lesson 60

A a
at*   as
and*   an*
am*

B b
big*   brother
biggest
be

C c
can*
children

D d
day*

E e
end*   eat*

F f
friend
float*

G g

H h
had*
has
he

I i
if   it*
in*   I
is

J j
jump*   jumping

K k
kittens

L l
little

M m
make*
me

N n
no
night*

O o
on
oil*
or

P p
pet*   player

Q q

R r
run*   ride*
red*   rain*

S s
so   see*
stop*
stopped
she
same*
skate*

T t
things*
this
to
those*
train*
the
there
tell*

U u
up   under
us   use

V v

W w

X x   Y y   Z z

Take-Home Word Wall
After Lesson 65

A a

at*   as
and*   an*
am*

B b

big*   brother
biggest
be

C c

can*
children
car*

D d

day*

E e

end*   eat*

F f

friend   for
float*

G g

H h

had*
has
he

I i

if   it*
in*   I
is

J j

jump*   jumping

K k

kittens

L l

little

M m

make*
me

N n

no
night*

O o

on
oil*
or
of

P p

pet*   player

Q q

R r

run*   ride*
red*   rain*

S s

so   see*
stop*   smart*
stopped sport*
she
same*
skate*

T t

things*
this
to
those*
train*
the
there
tell*

U u

up   under
us   use

V v

W w

X x   **Y y**   **Z z**

Take-Home Word Wall
After Lesson 70

A a
at*   as
and*   an*
am*   after

B b
big*   brother
biggest
be

C c
can*
children
car*

D d
day*

E e
end*   eat*

F f
friend   for
float*

G g

H h
had*   her
has   hurt
he

I i
if   it*
in*   I
is

J j
jump*   jumping

K k
kittens

L l
little

M m
make*   more*
me

N n
no
night*

O o
on
oil*
or
of

P p
pet*   player

Q q

R r
run*   ride*
red*   rain*

S s
so   see*
stop*   smart*
stopped   sport*
she   some
same*
skate*

T t
things*
this
to
those*
train*
the
there
tell*

U u
up   under
us   use

V v

W w

X x   Y y   Z z

Take-Home Word Wall
After Lesson 75

A a
at*   as   all*
and*   an*
am*   after

B b
big*   brother
biggest   because
be

C c
can*
children
car*

D d
day*

E e
end*   eat*

F f
friend   for
float*

G g

H h
had*   her
has   hurt
he

I i
if   it*
in*   I
is

J j
jump*   jumping

K k
kittens

L l
little

M m
make*   more*
me

N n
no
night*

O o
on
oil*
or
of

P p
pet*   player

Q q

R r
run*   ride*
red*   rain*

S s
so   see*
stop*   smart*
stopped   sport*
she   some
same*   saw*
skate*

T t
things*
this
to
those*
train*
the
there
tell*

U u
up   under
us   use

V v

W w
was
walk

X x   Y y   Z z

Take-Home Word Wall
After Lesson 80

A a
at*   as   all*
and*   an*
am*   after

B b
big*   brother
biggest   because
be

C c
can*   cloud
children
car*
could

D d
day*

E e
end*   eat*

F f
friend   for
float*

G g
girl

H h
had*   her
has   hurt
he

I i
if   it*
in*   I
is

J j
jump*   jumping

K k
kittens

L l
little

M m
make*   more*
me

N n
no   now*
night*

O o
on
oil*
or
of

P p
pet*   player

Q q

R r
run*   ride*
red*   rain*

S s
so   see*
stop*   smart*
stopped   sport*
she   some
same*   saw*
skate*   slow*

T t
things*
this
to
those*
train*
the
there
tell*

U u
up   under
us   use

V v

W w
was
walk

X x   Y y   Z z

Take-Home Word Wall
After Lesson 85

A a
at*   as   all*
and*   an*
am*   after

B b
big*   brother
biggest because
be

C c
can*   cloud
children
car*
could

D d
day*

E e
end*   eat*

F f
friend   for
float*

G g
girl

H h
had*   her
has   hurt
he

I i
if   it*
in*   I
is

J j
jump*   jumping

K k
kittens

L l
little   look*

M m
make*   more*
me

N n
no   now*
night*   new*

O o
on
oil*
or
of

P p
pet*   player

Q q

R r
run*   ride*
red*   rain*

S s
so   see*
stop*   smart*
stopped   sport*
she   some
same*   saw*
skate*   slow*

T t
things*   too (big)
this
to
those*
train*
the
there
tell*

U u
up   under
us   use

V v

W w
was
walk
when*

X x   Y y   Z z
zoo

Take-Home Word Wall
After Lesson 90

A a
at* as all*
and* an* are
am* after

B b
big* brother
biggest because
be

C c
can* cloud
children
car*
could

D d
day* dry*

E e
end* eat*

F f
friend for
float*

G g
girl

H h
had* her
has hurt
he

I i
if it*
in* I
is

J j
jump* jumping

K k
kittens

L l
little look*

M m
make* more*
me

N n
no now*
night* new*

O o
on over
oil*
or
of

P p
pet* player

Q q

R r
run* ride*
red* rain*

S s
so see* six
stop* smart*
stopped sport*
she some
same* saw*
skate* slow*

T t
things* too (big)
this
to
those*
train*
the
there
tell*

U u
up under
us use

V v
very

W w
was
walk
when*

X x Y y Z z
zoo

Take-Home Word Wall
After Lesson 95

A a
at* as all*
and* an* are
am* after

B b
big* brother
biggest because
be before

C c
can* cloud
children centers
car*
could

D d
day* dry*

E e
end* eat*

F f
friend for
float*

G g
girl
gym

H h
had* her
has hurt
he

I i
if it*
in* I
is

J j
jump* jumping

K k
kittens

L l
little look*

M m
make* more*
me my*

N n
no now*
night* new*

O o
on over
oil*
or
of

P p
pet* player

Q q
question

R r
run* ride*
red* rain*

S s
so see* six
stop* smart*
stopped sport*
she some
same* saw*
skate* slow*

T t
things* too (big)
this
to
those*
train*
the
there
tell*

U u
up under
us use

V v
very

W w
was
walk
when*

X x   Y y   Z z
zoo

Take-Home Word Wall
After Lesson 100

A a
at*	as	all*
and*	an*	are
am*	after	

B b
big*	brother	boy*
biggest	because	black*
be	before	

C c
can*	cloud
children	centers
car*	
could	

D d
day*	dry*

E e
end*	eat*

F f
friend	for
float*	

G g
girl
gym
glad*

H h
had*	her
has	hurt
he	

I i
if	it*
in*	I
is	

J j
jump*	jumping

K k
kittens

L l
little	look*

M m
make*	more*
me	my*

N n
no	now*
night*	new*

O o
on	over
oil*	
or	
of	

P p
pet*	player	probably

Q q
question

R r
run*	ride*
red*	rain*

S s
so	see*	six
stop*	smart*	said
stopped	sport*	
she	some	
same*	saw*	
skate*	slow*	

T t
things*	too (big)
this	
to	
those*	
train*	
the	
there	
tell*	

U u
up	under
us	use

V v
very

W w
was
walk
when*

X x   Y y   Z z
zoo

Take-Home Word Wall
After Lesson 105

A a
at*	as	all*
and*	an*	are
am*	after	

B b
big*	brother	boy*
biggest	because	black*
be	before	

C c
can*	cloud
children	centers
car*	creatures
could	

D d
day*	dry*

E e
end*	eat*

F f
friend	for
float*	

G g
girl
gym
glad*
green

H h
had*	her
has	hurt
he	

I i
if	it*
in*	I
is	

J j
jump*   jumping

K k
kittens

L l
little   look*

M m
make*	more*
me	my*

N n
no	now*
night*	new*

O o
on	over
oil*	
or	
of	

P p
pet*   player   probably

Q q
question

R r
run*	ride*
red*	rain*

S s
so	see*	six
stop*	smart*	said
stopped	sport*	
she	some	
same*	saw*	
skate*	slow*	

T t
things*	too (big)
this	they
to	then*
those*	their (car)
train*	
the	
there	
tell*	

U u
up	under
us	use

V v
very

W w
was
walk
when*

X x   Y y   Z z
zoo

178

Take-Home Word Wall
After Lesson 110

A a
at*   as   all*
and*   an*   are
am*   after

B b
big*   brother   boy*
biggest   because   black*
be   before   but*

C c
can*   cloud
children   centers
car*   creatures
could

D d
day*   dry*   do

E e
end*   eat*

F f
friend   for
float*

G g
girl
gym
glad*
green

H h
had*   her
has   hurt
he

I i
if   it*
in*   I
is

J j
jump*   jumping

K k
kittens

L l
little   look*

M m
make*   more*
me   my*

N n
no   now*   not*
night*   new*

O o
on   over
oil*
or
of

P p
pet*   player   probably

Q q
question

R r
run*   ride*
red*   rain*

S s
so   see*   six
stop*   smart*   said
stopped   sport*   snake*
she   some
same*   saw*
skate*   slow*

T t
things*   too (big)
this   they
to   then*
those*   their (car)
train*
the
there
tell*

U u
up   under
us   use

V v
very

W w
was
walk
when*
want

X x   Y y   Z z
zoo

Take-Home Word Wall
After Lesson 115

A a
at*	as	all*
and*	an*	are
am*	after	

B b
big*	brother	boy*
biggest	because	black*
be	before	but*

C c
can*	cloud
children	centers
car*	creatures
could	

D d
day*	dry*	do

E e
end*	eat*

F f
friend	for
float*	

G g
girl
gym
glad*
green

H h
had*	her
has	hurt
he	

I i
if	it*
in*	I
is	

J j
jump*	jumping

K k
kittens

L l
little	look*

M m
make*	more*
me	my*

N n
no	now*	not*
night*	new*	

O o
on	over
oil*	
or	
of	

P p
pet*	player	probably

Q q
question

R r
run*	ride*
red*	rain*

S s
so	see*	six
stop*	smart*	said
stopped	sport*	snake*
she	some	sweater
same*	saw*	scare
skate*	slow*	

T t
things*	too (big)
this	they
to	then*
those*	their (car)
train*	
the	
there	
tell*	

U u
up	under
us	use

V v
very

W w
was
walk
when*
want
were

X x   Y y   Z z
X x	Y y	Z z
	you	zoo
	your	

Take-Home Word Wall
After Lesson 120

A a
at*	as	all*
and*	an*	are
am*	after	

B b
big*	brother	boy*
biggest	because	black*
be	before	but*

C c
can*	cloud
children	centers
car*	creatures
could	

D d
day*	dry*	do

E e
end*	eat*

F f
friend	for
float*	

G g
girl	go
gym	get*
glad*	
green	

H h
had*	her
has	hurt
he	him*

I i
if	it*
in*	I
is	

J j
jump*	jumping

K k
kittens

L l
little	look*

M m
make*	more*
me	my*

N n
no	now*	not*
night*	new*	

O o
on	over
oil*	
or	
of	

P p
pet*	player	probably

Q q
question

R r
run*	ride*
red*	rain*

S s
so	see*	six
stop*	smart*	said
stopped	sport*	snake*
she	some	sweater
same*	saw*	scare
skate*	slow*	smaller

T t
things*	too (big)
this	they
to	then*
those*	their (car)
train*	them
the	
there	
tell*	

U u
up	under
us	use

V v
very

W w
was
walk
when*
want
were

X x   Y y   Z z
	you	zoo
	your	

Take-Home Word Wall
After Lesson 125

A a
at*	as	all*
and*	an*	are
am*	after	

B b
big*	brother	boy*
biggest	because	black*
be	before	but*

C c
can*	cloud
children	centers
car*	creatures
could	

D d
day*	dry*	do

E e
end*	eat*

F f
friend	for
float*	

G g
girl	go
gym	get*
glad*	
green	

H h
had*	her	how*
has	hurt	
he	him*	

I i
if	it*
in*	I
is	

J j
jump*	jumping

K k
kittens

L l
little	look*

M m
make*	more*
me	my*

N n
no	now*	not*
night*	new*	nice*

O o
on	over
oil*	
or	
of	

P p
pet*	player	probably

Q q
question

R r
run*	ride*
red*	rain*

S s
so	see*	six
stop*	smart*	said
stopped	sport*	snake*
she	some	sweater
same*	saw*	scare
skate*	slow*	smaller

T t
things*	too (big)
this	they
to	then*
those*	their (car)
train*	them
the	two (2)
there	
tell*	

U u
up	under
us	use

V v
very

W w
was	who
walk	with
when*	
want	
were	

X x Y y Z z
	you	zoo
	your	

Take-Home Word Wall
After Lesson 130

A a
at*	as	all*
and*	an*	are
am*	after	

B b
big*	brother	boy*
biggest	because	black*
be	before	but*

C c
can*	cloud
children	centers
car*	creatures
could	

D d
day*	dry*	do

E e
end*	eat*

F f
friend	for
float*	

G g
girl	go
gym	get*
glad*	
green	

H h
had*	her	how*
has	hurt	**have**
he	him*	**here**

I i
if	it*
in*	I
is	

J j
jump*	jumping

K k
kittens

L l
little	look*

M m
make*	more*
me	my*

N n
no	now*	not*
night*	new*	nice*

O o
on	over
oil*	**old***
or	
of	

P p
pet*	player	probably

Q q
question

R r
run*	ride*
red*	rain*

S s
so	see*	six
stop*	smart*	said
stopped	sport*	snake*
she	some	sweater
same*	saw*	scare
skate*	slow*	smaller

T t
things*	too (big)
this	they
to	then*
those*	their (car)
train*	them
the	two (2)
there	
tell*	

U u
up	under
us	use

V v
very

W w
was	who
walk	with
when*	**where**
want	**what**
were	

X x Y y Z z
	you	zoo
	your	

Take-Home Word Wall
After Lesson 135

A a
at*	as	all*
and*	an*	are
am*	after	

B b
big*	brother	boy*
biggest	because	black*
be	before	but*

C c
can*	cloud
children	centers
car*	creatures
could	come

D d
day*	dry*	do

E e
end*	eat*

F f
friend	for
float*	from

G g
girl	go
gym	get*
glad*	
green	

H h
had*	her	how*
has	hurt	have
he	him*	here

I i
if	it*
in*	I
is	

J j
jump*	jumping

K k
kittens

L l
little	look*

M m
make*	more*
me	my*

N n
no	now*	not*
night*	new*	nice*

O o
on	over
oil*	old*
or	our
of	

P p
pet*	player	probably

Q q
question

R r
run*	ride*
red*	rain*

S s
so	see*	six
stop*	smart*	said
stopped	sport*	snake*
she	some	sweater
same*	saw*	scare
skate*	slow*	smaller

T t
things*	too (big)
this	they
to	then*
those*	their (car)
train*	them
the	two (2)
there	
tell*	

U u
up	under
us	use

V v
very

W w
was	who	will*
walk	with	
when*	where	
want	what	
were	why*	

X x   Y y   Z z
	you	zoo
	your	

Take-Home Word Wall
After Lesson 140

A a
at*	as	all*
and*	an*	are
am*	after	

B b
big*	brother	boy*
biggest	because	black*
be	before	but*

C c
can*	cloud
children	centers
car*	creatures
could	come

D d
day*	dry*	do

E e
end*	eat*

F f
friend	for
float*	from

G g
girl	go
gym	get*
glad*	good
green	

H h
had*	her	how*
has	hurt	have
he	him*	here

I i
if	it*
in*	I
is	

J j
jump*	jumping

K k
kittens

L l
little	look*	like*

M m
make*	more*
me	my*

N n
no	now*	not*
night*	new*	nice*

O o
on	over
oil*	old*
or	our
of	

P p
pet*	player	probably

Q q
question

R r
run*	ride*
red*	rain*

S s
so	see*	six
stop*	smart*	said
stopped	sport*	snake*
she	some	sweater
same*	saw*	scare
skate*	slow*	smaller

T t
things*	too (big)
this	they
to	then*
those*	their (car)
train*	them
the	two (2)
there	that*
tell*	

U u
up	under
us	use

V v
very

W w
was	who	will*
walk	with	we
when*	where	went*
want	what	
were	why*	

X x
Y y
	you
	your

Z z
zoo

Making Words Take-Home Sheet

WORDO

W	O	R	D	O
		FREE		

Systematic Sequential Phonics They Use
Total Word List

ad	book	chew	day	faster	gate
after	bookshelf	chewing	deep	fat	get
Al	bore	chick	den	fathers	gift
all	boy	chicken	dens	fee	gifts
allow	Brad	child	destroy	fight	girl
am	brain	children	did	fin	glad
an	brat	chin	die	fine	gland
and	brew	chose	dine	fir	glory
ant	bribe	clan	dish	fire	glow
any	brick	clap	do	first	go
are	bride	clapping	dog	fist	goal
arm	brides	claw	doghouse	fit	goat
arms	bridle	cling	Don	fits	gold
art	brisk	clip	dot	flake	goo
as	broil	cloud	down	fleas	good
ash	brother	clouds	downstairs	fled	goon
asleep	brothers	clover	drain	flew	gown
at	bruise	coast	draw	float	grad
ate	bus	coat	drip	floating	grain
baby	but	coats	drop	floss	grand
ball	butter	cold	drown	flour	grandchild
base	butterfly	coldest	dry	flow	green
bat	by	come	dude	flu	greet
bats	cake	comets	due	flute	grin
be	came	commute	dug	fly	grind
beach	camp	commutes	each	foal	groan
because	camping	cook	ear	foil	group
bed	can	core	east	fool	grow
bee	cap	cot	easy	foot	growl
before	car	could	eat	football	growling
beg	care	cow	Ed	for	grunt
bend	carrots	crash	elephants	forest	gum
best	cars	crate	elf	form	Gus
bet	case	crater	end	fort	gym
bid	cash	crawl	ends	four	gymnasium
big	cat	crawls	enter	Fred	had
biggest	cause	create	escaped	free	ham
bit	cent	creatures	ever	fried	hand
black	center	crust	every	friend	hands
blackbirds	centers	cub	everybody	friendly	has
blast	chain	cube	everything	friends	hat
bled	characters	cue	exist	fright	have
blue	chart	cute	exit	frighten	hay
bluebirds	chase	Dan	face	frog	he
blur	chat	dancers	faint	from	heat
boats	cheat	dare	fall	fry	hen
body	check	dash	far	fun	her
boo	chest	date	fast		

Total Word List

here	last	motor	pan	question	Sam
hi	law	mow	parents	quiet	same
hide	lawn	mug	parrots	quit	sand
high	least	mute	part	quite	sandwich
highways	led	my	past	quote	sap
him	leg	name	Pat	rabbits	sat
hire	legs	names	paw	race	Saturday
his	lent	nap	pay	raft	saved
hit	let	neat	peach	rain	saw
ho	lick	neck	peanuts	raindrops	say
home	lid	Ned	peas	rake	scar
hook	lie	need	peck	ran	scare
hop	light	nest	pen	rat	scared
hopped	like	net	pens	rate	scat
horses	line	nets	pep	raw	scold
hose	link	new	pest	Ray	screen
hot	lip	newt	pet	reach	sea
house	lit	next	pets	ready	seat
how	little	nice	pig	red	secret
howl	loaf	Nick	pill	relay	see
hug	loan	nickels	pillows	rent	seed
hundred	look	night	pin	replay	seen
hundreds	lot	nip	plain	rest	seep
hunt	loud	no	plan	rice	sell
hurt	low	nod	play	rich	send
hurting	lug	nods	player	rid	sent
hut	lugs	nose	players	ride	set
I	mad	not	playground	rig	shade
ice	make	note	please	right	shaved
if	mall	notes	plow	ring	she
ill	man	now	plug	rip	shed
in	mane	nut	pockets	ripe	sheep
inch	many	nuts	pod	rise	shelf
ink	map	oats	pods	roast	shell
inn	market	of	pond	Rob	shine
into	Mars	oil	ponds	robe	ship
is	mat	old	pool	room	shook
it	mate	oldest	pop	rose	shop
jar	may	on	port	rot	shopped
jig	me	or	pot	row	shore
jug	met	other	pour	Roy	short
jugs	might	our	pow	rude	shot
jump	monster	over	pray	rug	show
jumping	moo	owl	present	run	showers
jungles	mooing	owls	pride	rust	shut
Kate	moon	oyster	pro	rut	shy
kin	more	pain	probably	sad	sick
king	most	paint	proud	said	side
kittens	mother	painters	prowl	saint	sift
lap	mothers	Pam	pry	salt	sing

Total Word List

sink
sir
sit
six
sixteen
skate
skater
ski
skin
skinny
sky
slack
slaw
sled
sleep
slice
slick
slid
slide
slow
slug
sly
small
smaller
smallest
smart
smear
smell
smother
snake
snap
sneak
snip
snow
snowball
snowflakes
snowplow
so
sock
soil
sold
some
something
soon
sore
sort
sour
soy
spa
Spain

speck
speed
spend
spent
spider
spill
spin
spoil
spoon
sport
spot
sprain
spray
spree
stab
stain
stall
stamp
stand
star
stare
start
stay
steady
steep
steer
step
stew
sting
stink
stir
stone
stop
stopped
store
strain
straw
strawberry
stray
string
stun
sub
Sue
sun
sway
sweat
sweater
sweaty
sweep
sweet

swing
swish
tab
take
takes
tall
tan
tar
tea
teach
teacher
Ted
teen
teeth
tell
ten
tent
test
that
the
theater
their
them
then
there
they
thin
thing
things
think
this
those
three
throat
tie
tile
till
Tim
tin
tire
title
to
toast
told
tomorrow
too
took
tool
top
tore

tow
toy
trace
track
trade
train
trains
tray
treasure
tree
trees
trick
Troy
true
trunk
trunks
trust
try
turn
turtle
twenty
two
under
uniforms
up
us
use
valentines
van
vase
vent
very
vest
vet
vine
vote
walk
walking
wall
want
was
way
we
weather
well
went
were
wet
what
when

where
whistles
who
why
wide
wig
wigs
will
win
wing
wings
wink
wins
wire
wish
wishes
with
wow
yard
yes
yesterday
yet
you
your
yourself
zoo
zoom
zooming

Systematic Sequential Phonics They Use
Reproducible Letter Cards

ⓐ	b	c	d	ⓔ
f	g	h	ⓘ	j
k	l	m	n	ⓞ
p	q	r	s	t
ⓤ	v	w	x	y
z				

E	D	C	B	A
J	I	H	G	F
O	N	M	L	K
T	S	R	Q	P
Y	X	W	V	U
				Z